Inhalants

DRUGS The Straight Facts

Alcohol

Antidepressants

Cocaine

Date Rape Drugs

Designer Drugs

Ecstasy

Hallucinogens

Heroin

Inhalants

Marijuana

Nicotine

Ritalin and Other Methylphenidate-Containing Drugs

■ DRUGS
The Straight Facts

Inhalants

Ingrid A. Lobo

Consulting Editor
David J. Triggle
University Professor
School of Pharmacy and Pharmaceutical Sciences
State University of New York at Buffalo

CHELSEA HOUSE
PUBLISHERS
A Haights Cross Communications Company
Philadelphia

CHELSEA HOUSE PUBLISHERS

VP, NEW PRODUCT DEVELOPMENT Sally Cheney
DIRECTOR OF PRODUCTION Kim Shinners
CREATIVE MANAGER Takeshi Takahashi
MANUFACTURING MANAGER Diann Grasse

Staff for INHALANTS

ASSOCIATE EDITOR Beth Reger
PRODUCTION EDITOR Megan Emery
ASSOCIATE PHOTO EDITOR Noelle Nardone
SERIES & COVER DESIGNER Terry Mallon
LAYOUT 21st Century Publishing and Communications, Inc.

A Haights Cross Communications ✦ Company

http://www.chelseahouse.com

First Printing

1 3 5 7 9 8 6 4 2

Library of Congress Cataloging-in-Publication Data

Lobo, Ingrid A.
   Inhalants/Ingrid A. Lobo.
      p. cm.—(Drugs, the straight facts)
Includes index.
Contents: An overview: what are inhalants?—History of inhalant use—
Properties of inhalants—How do inhalants act?—Abuse of inhalants—
Consequences of inhalant abuse—Trends and use of inhalants—Treatment
and prevention.
   ISBN 0-7910-7636-9
   1. Solvent abuse—Juvenile literature. 2. Solvents—Health aspects—Juvenile
literature. [1. Solvent abuse. 2. Substance abuse.] I. Title. II. Series.
HV5822.S65L63 2003
362.29'9—dc22
                                                        2003016779

Table of Contents

The Use and Abuse of Drugs

The issues associated with drug use and abuse in contemporary society are vexing subjects, fraught with political agendas and ideals that often obscure essential information that teens need to know to have intelligent discussions about how to best deal with the problems associated with drug use and abuse. *Drugs: The Straight Facts* aims to provide this essential information through straightforward explanations of how an individual drug or group of drugs works in both therapeutic and non-therapeutic conditions; with historical information about the use and abuse of specific drugs; with discussion of drug policies in the United States; and with an ample list of further reading.

From the start, the series uses the word *"drug"* to describe psychoactive substances that are used for medicinal or non-medicinal purposes. Included in this broad category are substances that are legal or illegal. It is worth noting that humans have used many of these substances for hundreds, if not thousands of years. For example, traces of marijuana and cocaine have been found in Egyptian mummies; the use of peyote and Amanita fungi has long been a component of religious ceremonies worldwide; and alcohol production and consumption have been an integral part of many human cultures' social and religious ceremonies. One can speculate about why early human societies chose to use such drugs. Perhaps anything that could provide relief from the harshness of life—anything that could make the poor conditions and fatigue associated with hard work easier to bear—was considered a welcome tonic. Life was likely to be, according to the seventeenth-century English philosopher Thomas Hobbes, *"poor, nasty, brutish and short."* One can also speculate about modern human societies' continued use and abuse of drugs. Whatever the reasons, the consequences of sustained drug use are not insignificant—addiction, overdose, incarceration, and drug wars—and must be dealt with by an informed citizenry.

The problem that faces our society today is how to break

the connection between our demand for drugs and the willingness of largely outside countries to supply this highly profitable trade. This is the same problem we have faced since narcotics and cocaine were outlawed by the Harrison Narcotic Act of 1914, and we have yet to defeat it despite current expenditures of approximately $20 billion per year on "the war on drugs." The first step in meeting any challenge is always an intelligent and informed citizenry. The purpose of this series is to educate our readers so that they can make informed decisions about issues related to drugs and drug abuse.

SUGGESTED ADDITIONAL READING

David T. Courtwright, *Forces of Habit. Drugs and the Making of the Modern World.* Cambridge, Mass.: Harvard University Press, 2001. David Courtwright is Professor of History at the University of North Florida.

Richard Davenport-Hines, *The Pursuit of Oblivion. A Global History of Narcotics.* New York: Norton, 2002. The author is a professional historian and a member of the Royal Historical Society.

Aldous Huxley, *Brave New World.* New York: Harper & Row, 1932. Huxley's book, written in 1932, paints a picture of a cloned society devoted only to the pursuit of happiness.

David J. Triggle, Ph.D.
University Professor
School of Pharmacy and Pharmaceutical Sciences
State University of New York at Buffalo

1

An Overview: What Are Inhalants?

"Their easy accessibility, low cost, and ease of concealment make inhalants, for many, one of the first substances abused."
—**Michele Spiess, Office of National Drug Control Policy (2001)**

Inhalants are a class of drugs that are familiar to all of us. They are useful chemicals in household products, and readily accessible in our homes and schools. Unlike some other abused drugs, such as cocaine, marijuana, and LSD, inhalants may be legally obtained. These chemicals have legitimate uses, and customers have, on the whole, unrestricted access to purchasing them. The ease of obtaining these products for use as drugs increases their abuse potential.

Chemicals whose vapors or gases can be intentionally inhaled to give the user a high are called inhalants. The use of inhalants produces psychoactive or mind-altering effects on the user. Inhalants are usually solvent fluids, a category that includes thousands of diverse chemicals. A few such chemicals and products that are abused are lighter fluid, markers, spray paint, and glue.

Inhalant abuse is also termed "volatile solvent abuse." It should be noted that many drugs besides those classified as "inhalants" can be administered by inhalation, including marijuana, cocaine, heroin, methamphetamine, fentanyl patches, and nicotine. These drugs are not volatile solvents and have different physical and chemical properties; therefore, they are not classified as "inhalants." Inhalants are chemicals that are volatile, meaning they can readily vaporize from liquid to gas state at room temperature. They are also solvents, meaning they have the ability to dissolve other substances. A third characteristic of inhalants is that they produce psychoactive effects after a user breathes in the chemical vapors.

Although classified together under a very broad category, different inhalants cause varied short-term effects and long-term consequences. They are classified together not based on associated chemical action, pharmacology, or toxicology, but because of the shared way these compounds are administered. This general term encompasses a vast number of products (over 1,400) that can be inhaled as drugs.

Abuse of inhalants is particularly predominant among young people. The Substance Abuse and Mental Health Services Administration's (SAMHSA's) National Household Survey on Drug Abuse (2001) revealed that in 2000 over 2 million Americans aged 12 to 17 had used inhalants at least once in their lifetime (Figure 1.1). Commonly termed "sniffing," "huffing," or "bagging," use of inhalants has a surprisingly high popularity among adolescents. Inhalants were the third most popular drug among preteens, after alcohol and cigarettes. Among high-school students, inhalants dropped to the fourth most popular drug of abuse (with marijuana moving ahead of inhalants). This survey found that an astounding 77,000 people aged 12 to 17 were in need of treatment for inhalant abuse.

Inhalant abuse was described as "a stepchild in the war on drugs" in the 1994 Research Report Series by the National Institute on Drug Abuse (NIDA).[1] The report noted that the dangers of inhalant abuse were not taken as seriously by the public in the "war on drugs," and not viewed in the same category of abuse as drugs such as alcohol, heroin, and cocaine.

Although inhalant abuse is a recognized world problem, inhalants are the least characterized and least studied of all drugs of abuse. What is it about inhalants that makes them less frequently talked about, and why are they taken less seriously

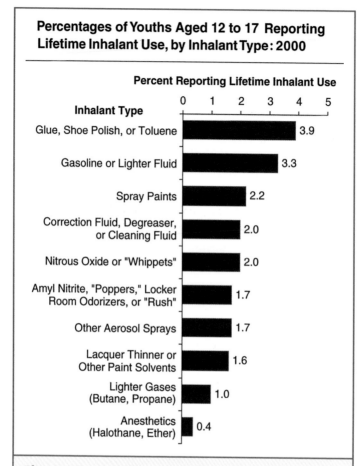

Percentages of Youths Aged 12 to 17 Reporting Lifetime Inhalant Use, by Inhalant Type: 2000

Percent Reporting Lifetime Inhalant Use

Inhalant Type

Inhalant Type	Value
Glue, Shoe Polish, or Toluene	3.9
Gasoline or Lighter Fluid	3.3
Spray Paints	2.2
Correction Fluid, Degreaser, or Cleaning Fluid	2.0
Nitrous Oxide or "Whippets"	2.0
Amyl Nitrite, "Poppers," Locker Room Odorizers, or "Rush"	1.7
Other Aerosol Sprays	1.7
Lacquer Thinner or Other Paint Solvents	1.6
Lighter Gases (Butane, Propane)	1.0
Anesthetics (Halothane, Ether)	0.4

Figure 1.1 Inhalants are the fourth most popular drug of abuse among high-school students. In 2000, more than 2 million Americans aged 12 to 17 had used inhalants at least once in their lifetime. In this graph, the inhalants are grouped by type. Volatile solvents were the most popular type of inhalant used, with 3.9% of individuals inhaling glue, shoe polish, or toluene.

than other drugs of abuse? Perhaps it is because young people abuse them more than adults. Perhaps it is because inhalants are so easy to find, are often viewed as a "low-status drug," and are legally obtained. All of these factors impact the way inhalants are looked upon by society. They are not viewed seriously as drugs by many, and the idea that inhalant abuse is a "childish fad" overlooks and trivializes its dangers.

Inhalant abuse can have very serious consequences. It can cause serious damage to the brain and nervous system. It can cause death by starving the body of oxygen and causing the heart to fail. It is unknown how many adolescents die each year from inhalant abuse because these deaths are often classified as deaths from suffocation, accidents, or suicide.[2]

The early signs of inhalant abuse often go unnoticed by parents, friends, and teachers. Inhalants are so cheap and seemingly harmless that abuse can go unrecognized. Additionally, the fact that the purchase of these products is legal leaves nothing in the way of obstacles for an inhalant abuser. Initial abuse of inhalants starts at an average age that is younger than that of abuse of either alcohol or tobacco. Research has suggested that inhalant abuse in young adults may be an indicator of continued and serious involvement with drugs later in life.[3] This makes inhalants a "gateway" drug, with use of inhalants predicting the use of other drugs later in life in some individuals.

Products that may be abused as inhalants do not always have a warning such as the "skull and crossbones" poison symbol on their label. However, any product with toxic ingredients includes a printed warning label similar to the following: "Intentional misuse by deliberately concentrating or inhaling the contents can be harmful or fatal." Products with this or similar warnings should be used in well-ventilated areas only for their legitimate purposes.

In spite of these warnings and the dangerous consequences of inhalant use, many users will still sniff for the high and the euphoria that drugs can induce. For instance, the philosopher William James found profound realizations of the religious experience after using nitrous oxide. He described some of these experiences in his book, *The Varieties of Religious Experience*, in 1902:

Nitrous oxide and ether, especially nitrous oxide, when sufficiently diluted with air, stimulate the mystical consciousness in an extraordinary degree. Depth beyond depth of truth seems revealed to the inhaler. This truth fades out, however, or escapes, at the moment of coming to; and if any words remain over in which it seemed to clothe itself, they prove to be the veriest nonsense. Nevertheless, the sense of a profound meaning having been there persists; and I know more than one person who is persuaded that in the nitrous oxide trance we have a genuine metaphysical revelation.

But James notes that not every experience with inhalants is profound or even pleasurable. In the same book, he quotes the physical, spiritual, and mental experiences and perceptions of J.A. Symonds after using chloroform:

After the choking and stifling had passed away, I seemed at first in a state of utter blankness; then came flashes of intense light, alternating with blackness, and with a keen vision of what was going on in the room around me, but no sensation of touch. I thought that I was near death; when, suddenly, my soul became aware of God, who was manifestly dealing with me, handling me, so to speak, in an intense personal present reality. I felt him streaming in like light upon me. . . . I cannot describe the ecstasy I felt. Then, as I gradually awoke from the influence of the anesthetics, the old sense of my relation to the world began to return, the new sense of my relation to God began to fade. I suddenly leapt to my feet on the chair where I was sitting, and shrieked out, 'It is too horrible, it is too horrible, it is too horrible,' meaning that I could not bear this disillusionment. Then I flung myself on the ground, and at last awoke covered with blood, calling to the two surgeons (who were frightened), 'Why did you not kill me? Why would you not let me die?' Only think of it. To have felt for that long dateless ecstasy of vision the very God, in all purity and tenderness and truth and absolute love, and then to find that I had after all had no revelation, but that I had been tricked by the abnormal excitement of my brain.

Symonds felt blankness, intense awareness, and religious ecstasy while under the influence of chloroform. But his feelings of joy did not last. Once the effect of the drug was gone, he felt the horror of extreme loss and disillusionment, realizing that he had been deceived by the "abnormal excitement" caused by the drug. As is clear from these two examples, users experience varied and even opposite responses to inhalants. Some feel euphoria and pleasure, while others experience sickness and depression. One example of the euphoric effects of inhalants is depicted in Figure 1.2. Nitrous oxide was used as a recreational drug during the 18th century at parties where participants would inhale the drug for its euphoric effects. The history of this drug will be described in greater detail in the next chapter.

The fact that there are so many different compounds abused as inhalants brings up question of how all of these compounds act on the brain. Do they all act in the same way? The answer to this question will be discussed in Chapter 4. It has been argued by some researchers that inhalant abuse should be regrouped as solvent abuse, volatile anesthetic abuse, and nitrite abuse, since the populations that abuse these substances are different.[4] Solvents are primarily abused by teenagers, anesthetics are generally abused by older professionals who have access to them, and nitrites are abused by populations older than teenagers. In the case of nitrites, as will be discussed later, the way the chemical acts upon the body appears to be quite different as well. In this book, the differences between these subgroups of inhalants will be discussed when useful.

Figure 1.2 The discovery of nitrous oxide led to its use as an anesthetic and recreational drug. Individuals held parties at which all the attendees would inhale nitrous oxide, which produced a state of excitement accompanied by laughter. Due to this reaction, nitrous oxide became commonly known as laughing gas.

Of all drugs of abuse, researchers know the least about inhalants. Many textbooks on drug addiction and pharmacology give inhalants a cursory glance or neglect to mention this category of drug altogether. Many surveys given to young people to determine their drug use omit questions on inhalants and solvents, and some only mention particular inhalants, such as glue.[5] This results in a set of incomplete information about inhalants. Many questions about inhalants remain unanswered.

The following chapters will include historical information on the discovery and use of inhalants. There will also be descriptions of the classes of inhalants and information given on many of the commonly abused chemicals. Explanations of the mechanisms by which inhalants act on the brain and body will follow, including the discussion of current research aimed at understanding drug addiction. The short- and long-term effects of inhalant abuse on the body will be described, and trends of inhalant use and attitudes toward it will be discussed. Lastly, there will be a presentation of information on treatment and prevention of inhalant use.

INHALANT FACTS

- Over 1,400 household products are abused as inhalants.
- Unlike many other drugs, the first use or experimentation with inhalants can be lethal.
- Inhalants are the least characterized and least studied of all drugs of abuse.
- Among preteens, inhalants are the third most-often-used drug.
- In 2000, more than 2 million people aged 12 to 17 reported using inhalants at least once during their lifetime.
- An estimated 141,000 people abuse or are dependent on inhalants.
- 77,000 people aged 12 to 17 are in need of treatment for inhalant abuse.

2

History of Inhalant Use

"But the prophetic current and breath is most divine and holy
[. . .] for when it is instilled into the body, it creates in souls
an unaccustomed and unusual temperament . . . it opens up
certain passages through which impressions of the future are
transmitted, just like wine, when its fumes rise to the head,
reveals many unusual movements and also words stored away
and unperceived."

—Plutarch, from
"Obsolescence of Oracles" in
Plutarch's Moralia, Volume V

THE ANCIENT GREEKS

The use of inhalants dates back at least as far as 1400 B.C.
At this time the Temple of Apollo at Delphi was founded on
Mount Parnassus in Greece. It was a place where people from
all over Greece would go to learn about the future and have their
most important questions answered about both politics and
private matters. The oracle of Delphi transmitted prophecies
first from the Earth goddess Gaia and later from the Greek god
Apollo. The oracle's shrine was built in the 8th century B.C. by
the Dorians, who considered Delphi to be the center of the Earth,
at its navel or "ompholos." Until A.D. 392, when the oracle was
banned by the Christian emperor of Rome, people would come to
the oracle to receive answers from a priestess called the Pythia.

Figure 2.1 Inhalants have been used for millennia, dating as far back as 1400 B.C. The ancient Greeks visited a priestess called the Pythia, pictured here (left), to receive answers about the future. The Pythia would breathe vapors and enter a trance, during which she told her prophecies to the listener. The vapors were most likely ethylene gas, which can stimulate the nervous system when inhaled.

This role was served by many women of unblemished character for nearly 2,000 years.

In the 1st century A.D., Plutarch, then the high priest at the temple, left records on how the oracle worked. He described the descent of the priestess into a small chamber where she would breathe divine, sacred vapors and enter a trance. Then the Pythia would return to sit on a stool with a basin of water held in one hand and a sprig of olive in the other and proclaim her prophecies from Apollo (Figure 2.1). The priest at the temple then wrote the response in verse form for the visitor.

Plutarch described the vapors as a "delightful fragrance coming on a current of air," and he believed they arose from a fissure or spring, possibly emanating from rocks disturbed by earthquakes. In 1927, scientists explored the area for a fissure or rising gas, and found nothing, so Plutarch's vapor idea was disregarded. It was revisited in 2001 when Jelle de Boer and his colleagues from Wesleyan University in Middletown, Connecticut, and the Kentucky Regional Poison Center discovered an unknown fissure carved by spring water that intersected a known fault immediately below the Temple of Apollo. They found evidence of methane (CH_4) and, more intriguingly, ethylene (C_2H_4) gases both in the spring and preserved within the rock under the temple.

Ethylene can be produced from methane, and any seismic activity along the fault would heat the spring and release the gases. Ethylene is a sweet-smelling hydrocarbon gas that can stimulate the central nervous system. Just 60 years ago, it was used as an anesthetic in hospitals. The gas is fatal in large doses, but in small doses it causes a disembodied sensation of euphoria, intoxication, and hallucination. Plutarch described some cases in which the Pythia would experience delirium, and comparing the experience to that of drinking wine, he noted that the intoxication was different from priestess to priestess. In one case he even described a death in the chamber when the priestess became hysterical and threw herself down, dying days later. The recent findings of de Boer and colleagues, demonstrating ethylene and methane gas emanating from a fissure beneath the Temple of Apollo, suggest that the priestesses, as part of their preparation and ceremony, were exposing themselves to inhalants and entering trances. This is an ancient example of inhalant use as part of a cultural and religious ritual.

ANESTHETIC GASES

In the 18th century, inhaled anesthetics were found to have mind-altering properties, and the enjoyable effects of these gases as recreational drugs led to their abuse. The anesthetic properties of these gases were noticed and, by the mid-19th century, medical use of these gases as drugs followed. Doctors and dentists found they could use these drugs to keep their patients from moving and feeling pain during operations. A discussion of three anesthetic gases—nitrous oxide, ether, and chloroform—follows, including information about their history, discovery, and early recreational and medicinal uses.

Nitrous Oxide

> "At the turn of the 18th century, Humphry Davy in England, experimenting with the newly discovered gas, nitrous oxide, discovered its mind-altering effects. He shared his find with friends at a succession of private parties. Later charlatans took the gas on the road, with traveling exhibitions at which for a fee, the audience might experience the effects of the gas."
>
> —Leo Hollister [6]

Nitrous oxide was originally discovered in 1776 by the English chemist Sir Joseph Priestley. Among his list of scientific accomplishments, Priestley isolated and described oxygen and carbon dioxide, found that graphite could conduct electricity, learned how to carbonate water ("soda water"), and invented rubber erasers. Priestley synthesized nitrous oxide (N_2O) by heating ammonium nitrate in the presence of iron filings and then passing the gas through water to purify it before storing it.

In 1799, Thomas Beddoes initiated an effort to use nitrous oxide and other newly discovered gases in medicine by creating the Pneumatic Institution. This was a private laboratory funded by private philanthropy, with a major contribution by

Josiah Wedgewood, the great English china manufacturer. He engaged a 21-year-old Englishman, Humphry Davy, to be the superintendent. Davy selected nitrous oxide as the first to investigate, announcing that he would inhale the gas himself, although it had been deemed poisonous by all prior investigators. Davy learned that inhaling nitrous oxide produced a state of excitement accompanied by loud laughter. This gave nitrous oxide its common name, "laughing gas." If he was in a relaxed state, inhaling the vapors induced sleep. According to Davy, "As nitrous oxide in its extensive operation appears capable of destroying physical pain, it may probably be used with advantage during surgical operations."[7]

The discovery of these pleasurable effects led to gatherings where invited guests would inhale nitrous oxide. On Davy's invitation list were many well-known individuals: the poets Samuel Taylor Coleridge and Robert Southey, Thomas Wedgewood (son of Josiah Wedgewood, who also worked with Davy in early experiments on photography), and Peter Mark Roget, who later wrote *Roget's Thesaurus*. Davy also noted that pains vanished under nitrous oxide's influence, proposing that it could be used in surgery in 1800.

Davy's hypothesis went untested for over 40 years. During the early decades of the 19th century, the medical community did not appreciate Davy's speculations about the possible anesthetic uses of nitrous oxide. Instead, nitrous oxide became a drug for recreational parties or "capers" where all the guests would inhale nitrous oxide. In the 1830s, nitrous oxide was a permanent exhibition to be shown, sniffed, and taken around for profit. For example, Samuel Colt, calling himself "Dr. Coult," took nitrous oxide on the road to raise the money to patent his now-famous revolver.

In 1844, a young American medical student named Gardner Quincy Colton decided to lecture on nitrous oxide and exhibit the effects of the gas after a fellow medical student suggested the idea to him. Colton's first demonstration thrilled him, leaving him with a profit of $400 over his expenses (today, this would equal around $9,500). With his huge success, he dropped out of school and started a nitrous-oxide business. Colton's "Grand Exhibitions" charged a 25-cent admission and provided 40 gallons of gas for those who wished to try it.

Horace Wells, a dentist, attended Colton's nitrous-oxide exhibition in Hartford, Connecticut, and noticed that when one of the audience members who had sniffed nitrous oxide tripped and cut his leg, he was astounded to feel no pain. Wells experimented the very next day by having a fellow dentist pull out one of his own teeth after Wells inhaled nitrous oxide. After awakening and feeling the empty hole where his troublesome wisdom tooth had been, Wells exclaimed, "It is the greatest discovery ever made. I didn't feel so much as a prick of a pin!" He had discovered anesthesia.

Wells used nitrous oxide on a number of his patients, and then introduced nitrous oxide during surgery at the

POPULAR ENTERTAINMENT

In Gardner Quincy Colton's advertisement for his nitrous-oxide demonstration, he described:

"A Grand Exhibition of the effects produced by inhaling Nitrous Oxid [sic], Exhilarating or Laughing Gas! Will be given at Union Hall this (Tuesday) Evening, Dec. 10th, 1844. . . . The effect of the Gas is to make those who inhale it either Laugh, Sing, Dance, Speak or Fight, and so forth, according to the leading trait of their character. They seem to retain consciousness enough not to say or do that which they would have occasion to regret.

N.B.—The gas will be administered only to gentleman of the first respectability. The object is to make the entertainment in every respect a genteel affair."

(from Edward M. Brecher's *Licit and Illicit Drugs*)

Massachusetts General Hospital in 1845. The first patient came out of anesthesia too soon, and Wells's discovery was not fully understood or appreciated. Wells continued his experiments with anesthetics and later became addicted to the anesthetic chloroform. Sadly, he committed suicide as a result of his chloroform addiction. Though nitrous oxide was not appreciated at its first public hospital demonstration, it is still widely used today as an anesthetic, particularly in combination with other volatile anesthetics during surgeries. Likewise, nitrous-oxide use as a recreational drug has continued from the early nitrous-oxide "capers" to the present day, with the use of whipping-cream-propellant "whippets" and nitrous-oxide balloons and canisters.

Ether

The Spanish chemist Raymundus Lullius learned of ether in 1275 from the Moors, who had brought the discovery to Spain. Lullius called it "sweet vitriol." In 1540, German botanist and apothecary Valerius Cordus described how to synthesize ether. Around the same time, a Swiss alchemist, scientist, and medical visionary named Philippus Aureolus Theophrastus Bombastus von Hohenheim (otherwise known by his adopted name Paracelsus) discovered ether's hypnotic effects. Paracelsus, who declared himself the "monarch of all the arts," also reintroduced opium to European medicine as laudanum, a mixture of opium and alcohol. For centuries this was the most effective painkiller available.

Ether ($C_4H_{10}O$) (Figure 2.2) is a liquid that vaporizes very quickly at room temperature. It can be either swallowed or inhaled, but the effects are faster by inhalation because inhalation is a more direct route to the brain. Friedrich Hoffman introduced ether into medicine under the trade name Anodyne in the early 18th century. It was described as "one of the world's most perfect tonics" and was prescribed for pains due to ailments as varied as kidney and gallstones, menstrual pains, intestinal cramps, earaches, and toothaches.

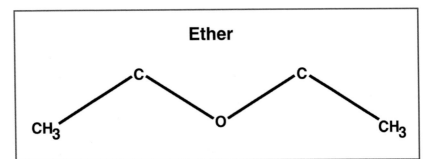

Figure 2.2 The chemical structure of ether is illustrated here. Ether is a linear molecule composed of carbon, hydrogen, and oxygen atoms. At room temperature, ether is a liquid that can vaporize quickly. Historically, ether was abused at times when alcohol use was prohibited.

In the 1790s, ether was often used as a recreational drug. Sniffing and drinking ether was popular at universities in the United States and England. Often ether was used as a substitute for alcohol. In the 1840s, wide-scale temperance movements were led in Ireland, England, and Scotland, and many alcohol abusers who wanted to maintain a pledge of abstinence from alcohol began to sniff ether instead. "Ether frolics" became popular and commonplace. Knowledge about ether from these recreational parties led to its use as a surgical anesthetic. On October 16, 1846, William Thomas Green Morton successfully administered ether at the Massachusetts General Hospital to a patient having a surgery to remove a neck tumor (Figure 2.3). Historians of anesthesia have named this day "Ether Day."

When the British government began to heavily tax alcohol in the 1850s, ether became even more popular. Whiskey was too expensive; ether was cheap, worked quickly, and could be used multiple times a day without a hangover (a condition characterized by a headache, discomfort, and sick feelings). By 1878, a surgeon visiting Draperstown, Ireland, remarked that the main street of the city smelled like his surgery, in which ether

Figure 2.3 Ether was used as a painkiller for centuries. In 1846, Dr. William T.G. Morton, pictured here, second from left, used ether on a patient during surgery as an anesthetic.

was used as an anesthetic. The hazards of ether abuse included deaths from overdoses and fatal burns from combining smoking with ether sniffing, as ether is highly flammable. By the 1890s, ether sales were regulated, but in spite of this ether abuse continued through the early 1900s.

Chloroform

Chloroform, which was discovered in 1833, was a third compound whose intoxicating properties were discovered before it was used as an anesthetic agent. Chloroform addiction was easily concealed, with addicts sniffing from a handkerchief throughout the day. The use of nitrous oxide, ether, and chloroform continue to a lesser extent today, occurring in some cases among anesthesiologists or other professionals who have become addicted to these agents.

GLUE

The 20th century brought a wide variety of new volatile compounds into everyday use. Most of these drugs are made through the distillation of petroleum, including glues and cements, gasoline, paint thinners, polish and spot removers, lighter fluids, paints, lacquers, enamels, and dry-cleaning products. Organic solvents in all of these compounds speed drying. Many of these drugs began to be abused during the 1920s, with use expanding during World War II and continuing to the present day. The intoxication from sniffing the vapors of these compounds resembles alcohol intoxication and in some instances produces mild hallucinations.

The use of glue as an inhaled drug goes back to at least the 1920s, but the practice was not documented in print until 1959, with publication of a report on glue-sniffing in the *Empire*, the Sunday magazine supplement of the *Denver Post*. Denver experienced a glue-sniffing epidemic that year. As a result, anti-glue-sniffing campaigns were launched and many young people were subsequently arrested for glue-sniffing.

Today, the abuse of inhalants is still a major problem. Inhalants are within easy reach, much as they were in the past. Additionally, in many cases they are still used as substitutes for other drugs that are illegal to purchase or too expensive to buy. These ties with the past use of inhalants makes further exploration of today's trends all the more interesting.

3

Properties of Inhalants

"Inhalants are the only abused substance classified solely by their means of administration—abusers take them by breathing in vapors from volatile substances. Thus, researchers must try to characterize a wide variety of substances and chemicals found in hundreds of common household, industrial, commercial, and medical products that can be inhaled to produce a psychoactive effect."

—Glen R. Hanson, Ph.D., D.D.S.,
NIDA Acting Director (*National Institute on Drug Abuse Notes*, November 2002)

TYPES OF INHALANTS

Inhalants are grouped into four categories: (1) volatile solvents, (2) aerosols, (3) anesthetics, and (4) volatile nitrites. Most of these compounds are very commonplace products that were never intended to be inhaled to achieve intoxication. Today, more than 1,400 products are used as inhalants.

Volatile Solvents

Volatile solvents include products as diverse as glue, paint thinners, degreasing compounds, dry-cleaning fluids, lighter fluid, gasoline, propane gas, refrigerant gases, correction fluids, felt-tip-marker fluid, electronic contact cleaners, and hundreds of other products typically used in the home and garage (Figure 3.1).

Figure 3.1 Common household products, such as the ones pictured here, can be abused as inhalants. These products, including aerosol room deodorizers, cleansers, lighter fluid, correction fluid, and nail polish, emit vapors that, when inhaled, can intoxicate an individual.

Aerosols

Aerosols comprise compounds such as spray paints, hair sprays, pain-relieving sprays, deodorants, fabric-protector sprays, vegetable frying-pan lubricants, and hundreds of other everyday chemicals that are found in homes or are readily available commercially. Products that create an aerosol use propellants to keep tiny particles suspended in the air. For the most part these propellants, not the liquid product, are the chemicals abused. Virtually any aerosol product can be abused.

Anesthetics

Anesthetics are a class of compounds used for medicinal purposes, such as chloroform, halothane, isoflurane, nitrous oxide, and ether, which have also been used as recreational drugs. Medically, anesthetic gases are used to create a loss of sensation and consciousness during surgical procedures. Abusers of inhalants use these compounds for the high they create. Often, abusers of anesthetics are professionals who have daily access to anesthetics. Anesthesiologists and dentists, who administer anesthetics to their patients, sometimes become abusers of their own drugs.[8] Nitrous-oxide tanks have been reportedly stolen and diverted for recreational parties (sometimes by students studying to be health professionals), and balloons of the gas are sold for recreational use.[9] The anesthetic gas nitrous oxide is also present in whipping-cream dispensers, chargers, and canisters which are commonly known as "whippets."

Volatile Nitrites

Unlike the other inhalants discussed, volatile nitrites do not act by depressing the central nervous system and slowing down the body. Volatile nitrites function as vasodilators and muscle relaxants. Vasodilators make blood vessels dilate, or become wider. This increases the heart rate. Amyl nitrite is used medicinally as a treatment for heart patients with angina.

These drugs are used recreationally in dance clubs where patrons sniff them on the dance floor to increase their enjoyment.[10] Combining the beat of the music, rhythm, light shows, and dancing with inhalant use makes the experience more enjoyable for some users. Nitrites were also commonly used in sexual pleasure, particularly by homosexual males during sexual activity to intensify the experience.[11] Unlike other inhalants, nitrite use has decreased considerably since 1979 among high-school students.

INTOXICATION BY INHALANTS

These different inhalants are abused by "sniffing," or inhalation by the nose, and "huffing," or inhalation by the mouth. They produce similar intoxicating effects, including dizziness, disorientation, and hallucination. The intoxication by inhalants is quick, with a short period of excitation followed by drowsiness, lightheadedness, loss of inhibition, and agitation. Often the effects of inhalation are interpreted as euphoric or pleasurable. The period of intoxication can last from a few minutes to a few hours, and is usually followed by a hangover or headache.[12]

It is suggested that the "high" experienced depends upon the emotional state of the user and his or her expectations. Users have reported hallucinations both frightening and pleasant, and they often contain symbolic content of personal significance to the sniffer.[13]

The following is an example of the mental processes during a rush of nitrous-oxide intoxication. The passage was written by the author William James in 1874 and reprinted in *The Atlantic Monthly*:[14]

> "What's mistake but a kind of take?
> What's nausea but a kind of -ausea?
> Sober, drunk, -unk , astonishment. . . .
> Agreement—disagreement!!
> Emotion—motion!!! . . .
> Reconciliation of opposites; sober, drunk, all the same!
> Good and evil reconciled in a laugh!
> It escapes, it escapes!
> But—
> What escapes, WHAT escapes?"

Under the effect of the drug, James would believe he understood religious mysticism, but when his high was gone, he was left with meaningless and confusing fragments and words. His experience had a cumulative effect on his thinking, culminating in his most acclaimed work, *The Varieties of*

Religious Experience, written in 1902.[15] The hallucinations, visions, and perceptions experienced when using inhalants can be psychologically and profoundly real to the user.

Additionally, intoxication by inhalants often results in uninhibited behavior similar to alcohol intoxication. Sniffers are sometimes mistaken for being drunk and in many cases have been arrested for intoxication.[16] This uninhibited and reckless behavior can result in accidents from poor judgment and impaired motor skills.

CHEMICALS IN INHALANTS

A vast number of the abused inhalants are organic solvents. Organic solvents are compounds composed of combinations of carbon, hydrogen, and oxygen atoms. Many abused organic solvents fall into a subclass of molecules called "hydrocarbons," meaning they are molecules made up of hydrogen and carbon atoms. They can be "aliphatic," which means they are noncyclic, straight or branched chains of atoms, or they can be "aromatic," which means the molecule has a ring structure. Some inhalants are inorganic compounds like nitrous oxide.

Some of the major types of abused chemicals in inhalants are discussed below. Unlike the properties of other drugs of abuse, the word "inhalants" encompasses many different types of chemical molecules that are grouped together because of their shared method of administration. Due to this broad classification, chemicals abused as inhalants are a large group of molecules.

Aromatic Hydrocarbons

Toluene (Figure 3.2a) is the principle intoxicant in many inhaled products and is one of the most frequently abused chemicals. Its chemical formula is C_7H_8, and it is a colorless, flammable liquid with a sweet, pungent odor. It occurs naturally in the tolu tree, in crude oil fuels, and from the distillation of coal tar. Toluene is used to boost the amount of octane in

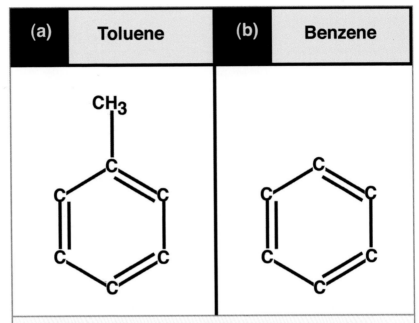

Figure 3.2 Toluene (a), an aromatic hydrocarbon, is in many inhaled products. The cyclic molecule has seven carbon atoms and eight hydrogen atoms. It is found in many paints, lacquers, adhesives, cosmetics, and perfumes. Benzene (b), another aromatic hydrocarbon, has properties similar to toluene, and is found in gasoline.

gasoline. The organic solvent is also present in many spray and house paints, correction fluids, paint thinners, fingernail polishes, lacquers, spot removers, glues, adhesives, cosmetics, epoxy resins, perfumes, and printing inks, as well as in gasoline and antifreeze.

There are other aromatic hydrocarbon molecules with properties like toluene. Benzene (Figure 3.2b) is found in gasoline, and xylene (not shown) is used in paints, paint thinners, and woodworking adhesives. Turpentine, widely used in oil-based paints and as a cleaning agent, has a high percentage of aromatic solvent. Another compound, white spirit, is used in paints and varnishes, and naphthalene is the aromatic component of moth balls. Aromatic hydrocarbons are highly soluble in lipids (fats), so they are readily absorbed by lipid-rich tissues in the body, such as the lungs, brain, heart, liver, and reproductive organs. These tissues concentrate the compounds shortly after inhalation, so the brain concentration of the compound can be 10 times higher than that in the blood.

Aliphatic Hydrocarbons

Aliphatic hydrocarbon compounds are found in lighter fluid and fuel gas, as well as in paint sprays, hair sprays, and air fresheners. These compounds are highly flammable and explosive. They include compounds like acetylene, butane, hexane, isobutene, and propane. Butane is often used as the propellant in aerosol sprays.

Hydrocarbon Mixtures

Gasoline and petroleum ethers are complex mixtures of chemicals. Gasoline may contain over 500 different hydrocarbons as a mixture of both aliphatic and aromatic hydrocarbons. Gasoline also contains additives, including toluene, benzene, ether, and alcohols. The primary components responsible for the euphoric effects of sniffing gas are the aliphatic hydrocarbons.

Along with being volatile, gasoline is well known to be inflammable and explosive. A number of other additives are present in gasoline, which adds to the toxicity of sniffing the mix of chemicals. One of these additives, lead, can be toxic to the body on its own and causes additional damage on top of the toxicity of the hydrocarbons themselves.

Halogenated Hydrocarbons

Halogenated hydrocarbons are hydrocarbons with halogen groups attached. Halogens are a set of elements in the periodic table (Group VIIA) that are characterized by their physical and chemical properties (Figure 3.3). A number of abused inhalants are halogenated compounds, containing fluorine,

Periodic Table of Elements

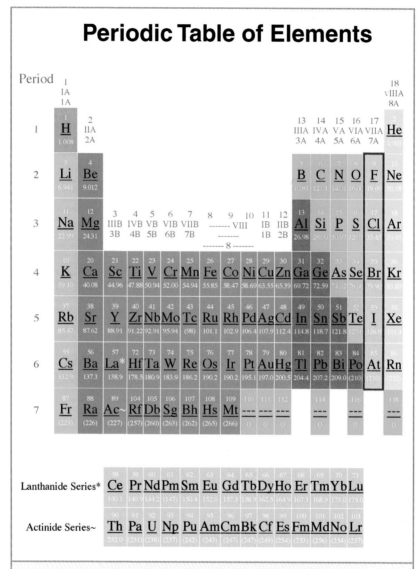

Figure 3.3 Group VIIA of the periodic table of the elements, shown here, contains the halogens, including the elements fluorine (F), chlorine (Cl), and bromine (Br). The halogens are nonmetals with strong, unpleasant odors that can burn flesh. One type of inhalant is the halogenated hydrocarbon where halogen atoms are attached to a hydrocarbon molecule.

bromine, and chlorine atoms. Halogenated compounds used as solvents are nonflammable and not explosive, and thus they are used in many household products used for cleaning and in fire extinguishers. Others are anesthetics, and some are used in air conditioners, refrigerators, and many aerosol sprays.

Trichloroethylene and 1,1,1-trichloroethane are used in correction fluids, dry-cleaning products, degreasing sprays, and solvents and spot removers. Bromochlorodifluoromethane is a compound found in halon fire extinguishers that is abused. Freon® is used for refrigeration and air conditioning systems. Anesthetics include halothane, chloroform, and the local anesthetic ethyl chloride. Methylene chloride is a component of rubber cement, paint strippers, and degreasing agents, and fluorocarbons are present in many types of aerosol sprays.

Ethers, Esters, and Ketones

Ethers, esters, and ketones are molecules containing carbon, hydrogen, and oxygen atoms. Ethers are colorless and have a sweet odor. Some ethers have anesthetic properties and are used medicinally. Enflurane, isoflurane, and sevoflurane are all ethers that are used clinically as anesthetics. Esters include ethyl and methyl acetate. They are used in various adhesives, gums, resins, waxes, and oils. Ketones are very effective solvents for fats, resins, and lacquers. Examples are acetone (the solvent in nail polish and nail polish remover) and methyl butyl ketone (widely used in paint thinners).

Nitrites

The nitrites include amyl, butyl, and cyclohexyl nitrite. They are all highly flammable, yellowish liquids. Amyl nitrite has been used since 1867 to relieve chest pain or discomfort due to heart disease, although it has been widely replaced by nitroglycerin. Originally, it was available in glass vials called pearls, designed to be opened with the fingers. The popping sound that resulted from snapping them open gave them the common names "poppers" and "snappers." Cyclohexyl nitrite is commonly found in room deodorizers and VCR head cleaners. Butyl nitrite, which was formerly marketed in room fresheners, is now an illegal substance.

Nitrous Oxide

Nitrous oxide has been used recreationally since Humphry Davy learned of its intoxicating properties in 1799. It is a small linear molecule that is a stable and colorless gas at room temperature. Nitrous oxide has been used clinically as an anesthetic since its early use in dentistry. Today, it is still commonly used in dental practices. Nitrous oxide is also used in combination with other anesthetics to facilitate changes in the depth of a patient's anesthesia. Because of its unique ability to enhance the uptake of a second anesthetic gas, it is often used in combination with anesthetics like halothane and isoflurane.

Use of nitrous oxide as a recreational drug occurs in high degree among medical and dental students of whom 10% to 20% have reported experience with the drug. Nitrous oxide is also commercially available as small cartridges of gas used by restaurants to make whipped cream. These are known colloquially as "whippets." Smaller volumes of nitrous oxide are found in whipped cream cans available in grocery stores.

PREFERENCE FOR INHALANTS

Over 1,000 products are abused as inhalants. Users may initially choose an inhalant because of its availability, but most indicate individual preferences for certain chemicals. Sniffers will often choose a specific product to abuse, be it a brand of glue, correction fluid, gold or silver spray paint, or whippets. In some regional areas toluene is the most popular inhalant; in others, gasoline and Freon.

Solvents are not always sniffed for their primary component. Hair sprays and paints are sniffed for the propellant gases that keep the main ingredient airborne when sprayed.

COMMON NAMES FOR INHALANT USE, ABUSERS, AND INHALANTS

TERMS FOR USING INHALANTS
Sniffing, Huffing, Snorting, Glading, Bagging, Chroming (inhaling paint fumes), Torch/fire breathing (igniting exhaled volatile gases, such as propane and butane).

INHALANT ABUSER
Huffer, Sniffer, Gluey (one who sniffs or inhales glue).

GENERAL NAMES FOR INHALANTS
Air blast, Bang, Bullet bolt, Discorama, Head cleaner, Heart-on, High ball, Hippie crack, Honey oil, Huff, Kick, Medusa, Moon gas, Oz, Poor man's pot, Satan's secret, Sniff, Toilet water, Whiteout.

COMMON NAMES OF SPECIFIC DRUGS

Amyl nitrite—Ames, Amies, Amys, Boppers, Pearls.

Amyl nitrite and Isobutyl nitrite—Poppers.

Isobutyl nitrite—Aroma of men, Bolt, Bullet, Climax, Hardware, Locker room, Rush, Rush snappers, Quicksilver, Snappers, Thrust.

Nitrous oxide—Buzz bomb, Laughing gas, Shoot the breeze, Whippets.

Octane booster—Toncho.

Rubber Cement—Snotballs (rubber cement rolled into balls, burned, and the fumes inhaled).

Toluene—Tolley, Texas shoe shine.

Gold and silver spray paints are preferred by some users for the solvents that keep the metallic particles suspended in the spray.

Some sniffers use inhalants indiscriminately and use a variety of products. Often household products have combinations of volatile chemicals in them, each of which produces a high on its own. This can make it difficult to identify whether a specific chemical or a combination of chemicals is responsible for subsequent behavioral changes and organ damage.

4

How Do Inhalants Act?

"Although inhalant abuse is now recognized as a worldwide problem, organic solvents are currently the least studied drugs of abuse. For example, relatively little is known about the underlying cellular mechanisms of action through which these substances produce their effects in the central nervous system."

—Madina R. Gerasimov (2002)
Brookhaven National Laboratory

INHALANT ENTRY INTO THE BODY

Inhalants enter the body through the nose or mouth (Figure 4.1). The human respiratory system works to bring oxygen into the body quickly. The lungs have a huge surface area and a rich capillary supply that rapidly and efficiently absorbs oxygen. When gaseous and volatile drugs are inhaled, they take advantage of this path, traveling through the lungs to the blood and reaching the brain in seconds.

SHORT-TERM EFFECTS OF INHALANTS

The immediate effects of inhalant abuse are similar to the classic early stages of anesthesia. The sniffer is initially stimulated, excited, disinhibited, and prone to impulsive or reckless behavior. He may also feel lightheaded and, with successive inhalations, less inhibited and less in control. The speech of the user becomes slurred and gait becomes staggered, with similarities to intoxication by alcohol. Euphoria, often accompanied by hallucinations, also may

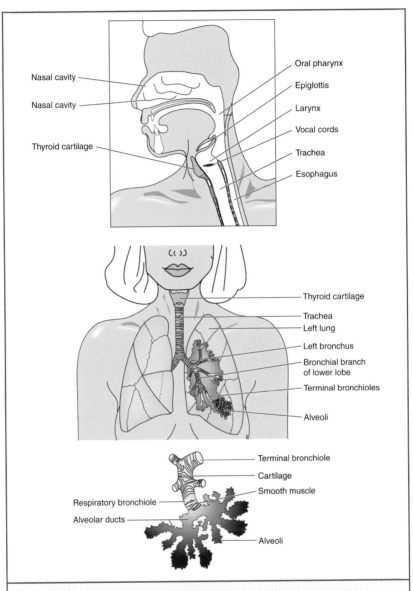

Figure 4.1 Inhalants enter the body through the nose or the mouth, and reach the brain more quickly when inhaled. The alveoli increase the surface area of the lungs and, consequently, make it easy for blood to become oxygenated. Substances that are inhaled untilize this pathway to reach the blood and then the brain quickly.

occur. This is followed by disorientation, muscle weakness, drowsiness, and sleep, most commonly after repeated cycles of inhaling the chemical.

THE BRAIN

The brain is a complex organ responsible for the coordination and regulation of all of the activities in life. Individual cells of the brain are called neurons (Figure 4.2). Neurons communicate with one another and with the rest of the body to allow us to think, feel, and perform physical actions. Inhalants and other drugs of abuse alter this basic and necessary communication between neurons to produce their effects, such as euphoria, hallucinations, and sedation.

There are approximately 100 billion neurons in the human brain. Neurons have wire-like processes called axons, which transmit information away from the cell, and processes called dendrites, which receive information from other cells. A single neuron's axon can transmit information to other cells over long distances (even four feet), while other neurons may transmit information short distances to neighboring cells. Axon endings make contacts on the cell bodies or dendrites of other neurons. The cell body is the part of the cell containing the nucleus. Neurons can have highly branched dendrites, on which axons from other cells can terminate, forming a synapse, where information can be communicated from one cell to the other.

All psychoactive drugs exert their actions on individual neurons in the brain; more specifically, drugs act on the contact points, or synapses, between cells. The synapse is the site of many important brain proteins, including ion channels (discussed later in this chapter) that are responsible for the rapid transmission of information between neurons.

Inhalants are central nervous system (CNS) depressants.[17] This means they slow down brain activity, which produces a calming and drowsy effect on the body. Other CNS depressants

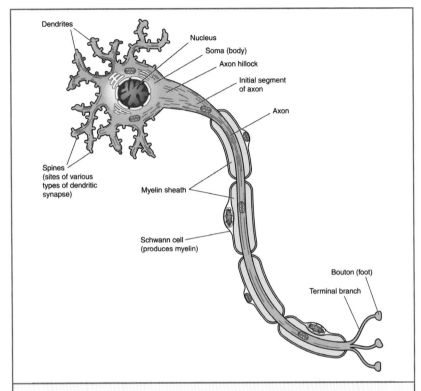

Figure 4.2 The brain has billions of cells called neurons. Each neuron, like the one shown here, has an axon that transmits information to other cells. The end of the axon, or the terminal branch, makes contact with the dendrites on other cells.

include narcotics, benzodiazepines, and barbiturates. The most widely abused CNS depressant is alcohol. All of these drugs have the potential to become both physically and psychologically addicting, and the mechanisms for the depressant effects of these drugs have been shown to overlap.

DISTRIBUTION OF INHALANTS IN THE BRAIN

Early studies on inhalants focused on the toxicity of exposure to inhalants, but made little progress toward understanding why abuse occurs and what the possible brain mechanisms underlying addiction to inhalants may be. Instead of looking at the brain, researchers had only looked at blood samples of inhalant abusers. Blood samples, however, do not provide insight into what inhalants do to the brain and why inhalants are addictive substances.

In 2002, researchers at the Brookhaven National Laboratory in Upton, New York, examined brain samples from living baboons and mice that were administered toluene, a chemical found in many inhalants that is known to have abuse potential. By radiolabeling carbon atoms in toluene, the researchers mapped out the distribution of toluene in the brain and body using a technique called positron emission tomography (PET).

Toluene was found to have a very rapid entry to the brain in both the primates and mice (within minutes). Since inhalants are lipophilic (fat-loving), they can enter the brain (which is over 50% fat) readily. In most areas of the brain, toluene was cleared quickly as well. This quick clearance from the brain is believed to account for why abusers repeatedly administer solvents. If the high from the drug begins and ends quickly, a user may be more prone to sniff again to achieve another high.

Toluene remained for longer periods of time in the lipid-rich white matter of the brain. The white matter of the brain contains axonal fibers only and no cell bodies. Some axons are myelinated, with a sheath of lipids that appears white, to speed transmission. Because toluene has a high uptake and low clearance from the white matter, this is an area that can suffer toxic damage from inhalant abuse. Damage and shrinkage of the white matter has been demonstrated in inhalant abusers. Inhalants were also found in the cerebellum, an area of the brain that is involved in motor coordination. Toluene is known to cause many malfunctions in behavior controlled by the cerebellum, resulting in an unsteady walk, muscle incoordination, and dizziness.

THE REWARD PATHWAY

Humans and other animals repeat behaviors because of their natural rewards. If doing something results in a pleasurable feeling, then this provides positive reinforcement to repeat that behavior. Naturally rewarding behaviors include eating, drinking, sex, and nurturing. These behaviors are necessary to survive, reproduce, and successfully raise offspring.

There is a reward pathway, or circuit, in the brain that positively reinforces pleasurable behavior (Figure 4.3). The reward circuit includes three areas of the brain that are interconnected with one another: the ventral tegmental area (or VTA), the nucleus accumbens, and the prefrontal cortex. Axons from neurons in the VTA communicate with neurons in the other two areas via the reward pathway.

When the brain receives a rewarding stimulus, a chemical messenger called dopamine is released by VTA neurons. Dopamine affects neurons of the nucleus accumbens and the prefrontal cortex, and its release is associated with a feeling of pleasure and reward. Scientists can measure an increased release of dopamine in the reward pathway after a rat receives a reward.[18]

WHY ARE INHALANTS ADDICTIVE?

The use of drugs can also cause a feeling of reward via the same pathway that natural rewards activate, causing dopamine release. Inhalants are addictive because they stimulate the reward circuit of the brain. Because drugs can act like natural rewards, they can hijack the reward pathway and lead to addiction. Addiction occurs when an individual engages in a compulsive behavior, even when faced with negative consequences. This behavior is reinforcing, or rewarding. One major feature of addiction is the loss of control in use of the addictive substance, making addiction a disease with both physical and psychological manifestations.

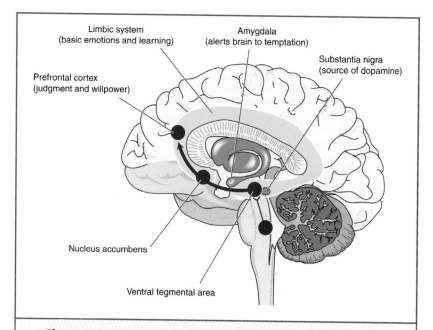

Limbic system
(basic emotions and learning)

Amygdala
(alerts brain to temptation)

Substantia nigra
(source of dopamine)

Prefrontal cortex
(judgment and willpower)

Nucleus accumbens

Ventral tegmental area

Figure 4.3 The reward pathway is the pathway in the brain that positively reinforces pleasurable behavior. When the brain receives a rewarding stimulus, the neurons in the ventral tegmental area release dopamine. The dopamine, in turn, affects neurons in the nucleus accumbens and the prefrontal cortex.

Scientists investigating drugs and the reward system learned a great deal from studies with rats. Because the chemistry of the human brain and that of the rat brain are similar, they believe that the process of drug addiction may be the same for both. Other animals, such as nonhuman primates, are also studied by addiction researchers because these animals can also become addicted to drugs of abuse like humans, and this addiction can be studied in the laboratory.

In 2002, Madina Gerasimov and colleagues at the Brookhaven National Laboratory found that inhalation of a behaviorally relevant concentration of toluene (the amount a sniffer would use) caused an increase in dopamine release in the brains of freely moving rats. Toluene inhalation combined with cocaine administration caused a huge increase in the release of dopamine in the nucleus accumbens. The measured dopamine released was much more than the amount of dopamine released after use of toluene alone plus the release after cocaine alone. This may account for why so many inhalant users abuse multiple addictive drugs. The effect of using two or more drugs simultaneously may result in an even more pleasurable experience for these individuals.

Another study in rats found that toluene activated dopamine neurons in the reward pathway. Inhaled toluene caused activation of dopamine neurons and caused hyperactive movement (with less movement at high doses). Adding toluene to rat brain neurons caused them to have increased activity.[19] These results are further evidence that inhalants, such as toluene, lead to addiction by activating the reward pathway. Answering the question of why this activation occurs is a current area of study.

SITES OF ACTION OF INHALANTS

Inhalants have such similar behavioral consequences to other central nervous system depressants that scientists have looked to see if inhalants have similar mechanisms of action. For some drugs of abuse, specific receptors are the initial target of the drug. Examples where the target receptors are known include the opioid receptors for drugs like opium, heroin, and morphine and the cannabinoid receptors for marijuana. Inhalants are more similar to alcohol, which produces multiple changes to cells and acts in a more complex, and thus less understood, manner. Like alcohols, volatile solvents and anesthetics were initially believed to disrupt the membranes surrounding cells in a nonspecific manner. This view has changed in the past 20 years. Today there is evidence that these drugs all have direct effects on proteins, particularly those in the brain. Ion channel proteins have been identified as critical for volatile anesthetic action.

INHALANTS AND ION CHANNELS

Ion channels are tunnel-shaped proteins that span the cell membrane and act as pores. The channels have gates that open and close to allow ions to move into or out of a cell (Figure 4.4). Ions, such as chloride, sodium, potassium, and calcium, are atoms that have gained or lost one or more electrons to give them either a positive or negative electrical charge. Ions are unequally distributed inside and outside the neuronal membrane, creating a negative charge inside and a positive charge outside the cell. When an ion channel opens, millions of ions can rush in and out of the cell each second due to their unequal distribution. This results in an electrical signal, or current, which is the basis of the rapid communication between neurons.

An important function of ion channels is to regulate when cells are at rest and when they are communicating. They generate the electrical signals that make our hearts beat, our muscles contract, and perhaps most importantly, allow our brains to receive and process information. This communication between cells allows for orchestration of our physical and mental activities. Normal brain function results from the balance of excitatory and inhibitory signals that neurons receive via ion channels, and drugs can throw off this normal balance. Researchers have found that a number of ion channels have altered functions in the presence of commonly abused inhalants (for example, toluene and 1,1,1-trichloroethane). These channels include the NMDA, GABA, and glycine receptors. Receptors are proteins on the cell membrane to which chemical messengers called neurotransmitters bind. Two neurons can communicate when one releases a neurotransmitter, which binds to receptors for that neurotransmitter on another cell, resulting in the opening of ion channels.

NMDA receptors bind glutamate, the major excitatory neurotransmitter in the brain. NMDA receptors regulate how excited or stimulated the nervous system is and they are also involved with learning and memory processes. Silvia L. Cruz,

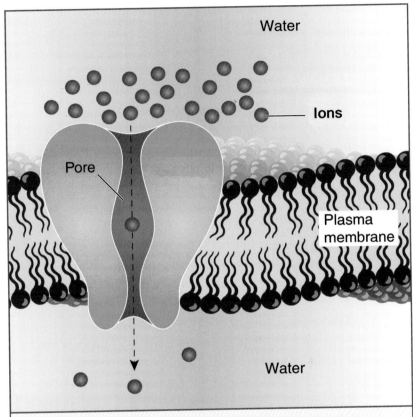

Figure 4.4 Ion channels, proteins on the cell membrane, act as gates that allow ions, such as sodium and potassium, through the plasma membrane. The pores open and close to regulate the movement of ions and, thus, the communication between neurons.

John J. Woodward, and colleagues found that NMDA receptors were affected by volatile solvents. They found that the particular form of the receptor most predominantly expressed in the brain during adolescence is the most sensitive to inhalants. This could have serious implications, since inhalant abusers are most often adolescents, and this may partially explain the impaired cognition and learning functions noted in inhalant abusers.

GABA and glycine receptors are major inhibitory neuro-transmitter receptors that are involved with decreasing neuronal activity. These receptors were shown by Michael J. Beckstead, S. John Mihic, and colleagues (from Wake Forest University School of Medicine, University of California at San Francisco, and the University of Texas at Austin) to be enhanced by inhaled drugs of abuse in the same manner as other central nervous system depressants. Researchers found that the sites of action of inhaled solvents on these ion channels may overlap sites of action of other CNS depressants. They also showed that ethanol, volatile anesthetics, and solvents can compete with one another to produce changes in glycine receptor function. This is convincing evidence that these drugs may all act in a similar way on this receptor (and possibly other receptors) to produce their effects.

NITRITES AND THEIR TARGETS

The main pharmacological site of action of nitrites is on smooth muscles, such as the linings of the digestive organs, air passages of the lungs, and the walls of blood vessels. Volatile nitrites relax the smooth muscles, particularly those of the blood vessels. This leads to pooling of blood and results in a

HOW INHALANTS AFFECT THE BODY

- Inhalants enter the body via the lungs and reach the brain in seconds.

- Most inhalants are central nervous system depressants.

- Inhalants are addictive because they activate the brain's reward pathway.

- Inhalants change the way ion channels function and can change the way neurons in the brain communicate.

- Volatile nitrites act differently from other inhalants because they relax smooth muscles.

dramatic drop in blood pressure. The user experiences a sense of warmth, giddiness, throbbing sensations, a pounding heart, and flushing of the face and chest.

Direct central nervous system effects of volatile nitrites have not yet been determined. In the body, nitrites are rapidly broken down into alcohol and nitrite ions, so the parent nitrite drugs may not reach the brain in concentrations comparable to those found in the blood. In one study, isoamyl nitrite concentrations were measured in the brains of rats exposed to the compound by inhalation. The drug was found to inhibit the synthesis or release of some adrenal steroids in the hypothalamus that are involved with stress. To understand the abuse potential of volatile nitrites, many more studies are needed to establish direct effects of the drugs on the brain.

FUTURE STUDIES

One of the major problems with why inhalants are so poorly understood is that little scientific focus has been aimed at understanding how inhalants affect the brain and behavior. Previous research on inhalants has focused more on organ toxicity caused by inhalants, the trends in inhalant use, and their anesthetic functions. Understanding inhalant abuse at the cellular and molecular level has been a neglected field. Since there have been a number of studies on the cellular basis for inhalant abuse in the past five years, this is hopefully an indication that future research will focus more on this area.

5

Abuse of Inhalants

"Most inhalants are commercial products composed of a variety of chemicals. Each of these chemicals carries its own potential for toxic damage to vital organ systems. When the multiple toxic ingredients act together, a multiplied, synergistic in-vivo toxicity can be projected. This toxic impact is then augmented by the typical developmental immaturity of the user, the massive concentrations of these substances achieved in abuse settings, the efficiency of the lungs at delivering these toxic chemicals to vital tissues at high concentrations, and the tendency for lipid-rich vital organs to avidly retain these lipid-like organic toxins. The summation of these and yet other factors confers upon inhalants as a class a more formidable toxic profile than any other type of drug of abuse."

—**National Inhalant Prevention Coalition**

INHALANT ADMINISTRATION

Inhalants are abused by a number of different methods. "Sniffing" involves breathing the chemical vapors through the mouth. Some users sniff directly from an open container of the product or spray a product in an empty soft-drink can and inhale, while others may paint their fingernails with a substance and sniff it throughout the day. "Bagging" is another method of administration, in which the user places inhalants such as glue or gasoline in a plastic bag. The user then holds the bag to his face and inhales the fumes (Figure 5.1). Nitrous oxide, for example, is often inhaled from a balloon. "Huffing" involves soaking a cloth with the chemical, placing the cloth in the mouth and inhaling the fumes. Another method of administration is spraying the chemical directly into the oral cavity. This method is often used to administer aerosols.

WHY DO PEOPLE ABUSE INHALANTS?

The reasons for inhalant abuse vary from individual to individual. Abusers usually begin their inhalant use because they enjoy the high and euphoria they experience from the drug use. They continue to use drugs because of a number of different factors that differ from user to user. Some of these factors include the affordability and availability of the drugs, environmental influences, and boredom. Others abuse the drugs because they give fast and multiple highs, or to alleviate stress. One example of this is a quote from an inhalant abuser in a study by Reyes Ramos and the Texas Commission on Alcohol and Drug Abuse:

> I was twenty-four and divorced when I got started. I met this guy, and he told me that the spray would help take my worries away. You know, I was all depressed and everything, so I tried it. I liked it and started doing it all the time, but it didn't take my worries away. The spray made it worse. I lost my kids and everything. They are still in foster homes and everything, and I'm all messed up . . . [20]

Young abusers may use inhalants to express rebellion, they may be influenced by their peers, have a lack of parental guidance, or find inhalants easier to hide from or explain to parents than other drugs like alcohol or marijuana. Possibly, their friends and siblings approve of or promote drug use. In the long run, abusers of inhalants become addicted and dependent on the drugs of abuse and need to continue abusing them.

TYPES OF INHALANT ABUSERS

Abusers of inhalants were classified into three categories by Oetting and colleagues of Colorado State University in

Figure 5.1 Many individuals use inhalants for a variety of reasons. This young boy from Cambodia is inhaling glue from a plastic bag.

1988: (1) inhalant-dependent adults, (2) polydrug users, and (3) young inhalant users. Inhalant-dependent adults have the most serious health problems because of their long-term use and dependence on chemicals. These users may also abuse other drugs, but they prefer using inhalants. Some of these abusers

Alcohol or Drug Abuse Among Adolescent Inhalant Admissions: 1999

Other Drugs Abused	Percent
Both Alcohol and Marijuana	53.5
Marijuana Only	12.1
Marijuana and a Drug Other Than Alcohol	11.9
Alcohol Only	6.3
Alcohol and a Drug Other Than Marijuana	4.1
Other Drugs/Drug Combinations	2.7
None (Abused Inhalants Only)	9.4
Total	100.0

Figure 5.2 Users of inhalants may become dependent or may also begin to use other drugs. The table above shows that among adolescents who use inhalants, most abuse other drugs, such as alcohol and marijuana.

include health-care professionals who have access to anesthetics, or are individuals who have been using inhalants for many years. Polydrug users use inhalants, as well as other drugs (Figure 5.2). They may prefer another drug over inhalants and still use inhalants, or they may enjoy combining the high from inhalants with that of another drug. The young inhalant users are in their experimentation period with inhalants (Figure 5.3). They may fall into either of the other two categories with time, with some young inhalant users becoming lifetime users and some becoming polydrug users. The young inhalant users are

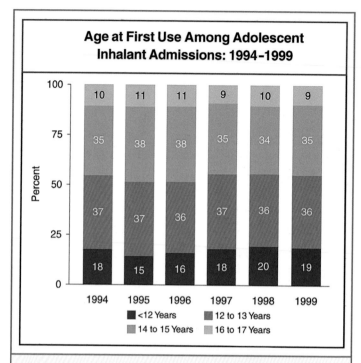

Age at First Use Among Adolescent Inhalant Admissions: 1994–1999

Figure 5.3 First-time inhalant users are most often youth. The chart above shows the age at which adolescent patients admitted for treatment first used inhalants between 1994 and 1999. Treatment and prevention programs are most often focused on adolescents.

the individuals that treatment is most often focused on because these users are the largest group. Also, intervention is more likely to be successful when drug use is caught early on.

FREQUENCY OF INHALANT USE

Inhalant users interviewed in treatment facilities had high frequencies of use, with 60% reporting daily current use of inhalants and an additional 14% reporting use more than once every week.[21] These statistics reveal that users are dependent on inhalants (dependence is discussed in greater detail later in this chapter).

DIAGNOSTIC CRITERIA

Dependence and addiction to drugs of abuse have different characteristics in different individuals. The diagnostic criteria for inhalant dependence and addiction have been defined by the fourth edition of the Diagnostic and Statistical Manual of Mental Disorders (DSM-IV). DSM-IV is published by the American Psychiatric Association and is used as the main diagnostic reference by mental-health professionals in the United States. The diagnostic criteria for inhalant dependence and addiction are as follows:

A maladaptive pattern of substance use, leading to clinically significant impairment or distress, as manifested by three (or more) of the following, occurring at any time in the same 12-month period.

(1) Tolerance, as defined by either of the following:

(a) a need for markedly increased amounts of the substance to achieve intoxication or desired effects

(b) markedly diminished effect with continued use of the same amount of the substance

(2) Withdrawal, as manifested by either of the following:

(a) the characteristic withdrawal syndrome for the substance

(b) the same (or closely related) substance is taken to relieve or avoid withdrawal symptoms

(3) The substance is often taken in larger amounts or over a longer period than was intended

(4) There is a persistent desire or unsuccessful efforts to cut down or control substance use

(5) A great deal of time is spent in activities necessary to obtain the substance (e.g., visiting multiple doctors or driving long distances), use the substance (e.g., chain smoking), or recover from its effects

(6) Important social, occupational, or recreational activities are given up or reduced because of substance abuse

(7) The substance use is continued despite knowledge of having a persistent or recurrent physical or psychological problem that is likely to have been caused or exacerbated by the substance (e.g., current cocaine use despite recognition of cocaine-induced depression, or continued drinking despite recognition that an ulcer was made worse by alcohol consumption).

TOLERANCE

Heavy abuse of inhalants leads to tolerance, a situation in which users need to inhale a greater and greater amount of chemicals to get the same high they used to get from smaller amounts. The development of tolerance is common with addictions to other drugs such as alcohol. Following a year of regular and heavy use, a glue sniffer may use eight to 10 tubes of glue to reach the same high that a single tube initially produced. One serious case reported in Germany described an adult male who was an inhalant abuser. He abused propane and compensated for the tolerance he had developed by continuing to increase the dose he sniffed to a massive consumption of five liters of propane daily.[22]

SENSITIZATION

In some cases, inhalant abusers display sensitization to the drugs they are using. This means they become more sensitive to the drug's effects at lower doses. In these cases, a smaller amount of the drug is necessary to produce the same effect.

ADDICTION

Addiction is a disease that stems from the need for and reliance on a drug. It can begin with a simple initiation. An individual decides to try using a drug. For inhalants, he may sniff a marker, glue, or gasoline after being introduced to the inhalant by a friend, or discovering it on his own. After initiation to this experience, the user may return to the drug again if the experience was pleasurable. The odor of the drug, the excitement of doing something illicit, and the high the user experiences

PHYSICAL AND BEHAVIORAL SIGNS OF INHALANT ABUSE

Inhalant abuse may be recognized by both physical and behavioral signs. Some of these behaviors are mistaken for drunkenness, and many of the physical signs can be mistaken or go unnoticed. The most-often-recognized sign is the smell of chemicals on the breath. Signs of inhalant use include the following:

PHYSICAL	BEHAVIORAL
Chemical odors on hair and clothing	Drunk or dazed appearance
Smell of chemicals on breath	Lack of coordination/dizziness
Empty spray cans or bottles	Slurred speech
Hidden glue bottles or aerosols	Apathetic behavior and depression
Hidden chemical-soaked rags	Aggressiveness and violent behavior
Paint stains on clothing or skin	Inability to concentrate or inattentiveness
Red eyes	Anxiety
Nosebleeds, red or runny nose	Loss of appetite, weight loss (long term)
Sores around the mouth and nose	Nausea
Pupils either constricted or dilated	Excitability
Fast, deep, or labored breathing	Impaired vision
Neglect of personal appearance/hygiene	Fatigue
	Memory loss

can add to this initiation and can create a positive impression of the drug. The individual may try using the drug again and again. Inhalant abuse falls into this category. At a certain point, addiction occurs. The user feels the need for the drug in order to be happy, and he begins overlooking his family, friends, and job. The drug becomes the user's one priority. Addiction puts the individual at risk of losing the things that are dear to him and can permanently damage his health.[23]

Inhalants have a very serious abuse potential that is often overlooked or downplayed. In 1998, estimates generated from the National Household Survey on Drug Abuse calculated that every 46 seconds someone in the United States abuses an inhalant for the first time. This number is very near the estimate for cocaine (43 seconds). Though inhalant abuse is often less recognized, as Chapter 7 describes, it is no less dangerous than other forms of substance abuse.

Not all individuals who try inhalants will become addicted. Some will not even enjoy the experience. Why some users enjoy the use of inhalants and continue using them and others do not is unknown. Researchers also do not know why some recreational drug users become addicted to inhalants and others do not. Addiction has both genetic and environmental components, so it is most likely that these factors play a role in determining who becomes addicted to a drug and who does not.

DEPENDENCE AND WITHDRAWAL

Chronic use of inhalants can lead to the body's physical need for a drug, which is called dependence. Addiction is a psychological and physical disease, and dependence is a physical manifestation of the disease. The body adapts to the presence of the drug, and heavy users experience withdrawal if they stop using inhalants abruptly. Withdrawal symptoms indicate an abuser is physically dependent on inhalants. These symptoms have been reported to occur in approximately 50% to 60% of inhalant users. When they quit inhaling, withdrawal symptoms appear. The body has to adapt to the fact that the drug is gone. Withdrawal symptoms generally begin within hours to a few days after the user stops using inhalants, and in some cases may not appear for a full week.

Withdrawal symptoms include depression, aggression, restlessness, irritability, shaking, headaches, chills, anxiety, sweating, nausea, abdominal pains, and a lack of energy. In the most severe cases, a delirium tremens-like syndrome has been observed, including symptoms of tremors, increased irritability, sleeping disorders, and hallucinations.[24] Addicted users may then return to the drug to eliminate their withdrawal symptoms and be unable to quit using the drug.

Dependence upon inhalants is known to develop in some users. The users feel an urgent need for inhalants and anxiety when they do not get the substance. Humphry Davy, who discovered the intoxicating properties of nitrous oxide, described that it could lead to a state of dependency:

> . . . a desire to breathe the gas is always awakened in me by the sight of a person breathing, or even by that of an air-bag or an air-holder . . . From the strong inclination of those who have been pleasurably affected by the gas to respire it again, it is evident that the pleasure produced is not lost, but that it mingles with the mass of feelings, and becomes intellectual pleasure or hope. The desire of some individuals acquainted with the pleasure of nitrous oxide for the gas has been so strong as to induce them to breathe with eagerness, the air remaining in the bags after the respiration of others.[25]

Most inhalant abusers have tried to but are unable to quit, and have reported this to treatment facilities.[26] In spite of knowing the adverse consequences of their continued use, addicted individuals continue using inhalants. Relapse into use of the drug because of withdrawal symptoms and desire for the drug can prevent addicted users from quitting.

6

Consequences of Inhalant Abuse

"A drug user's knowledge, if adequate, lets him or her, identify unwanted side effects and deal with them in a self-satisfactory way. Users concentrating on a desired main effect may not observe an unpleasant side-effect or may not connect it with use of the drug."

—H.S. Becker [27]

ORGAN DAMAGE

The abuse of inhalants can cause irreversible damage to the body. Organ damage and other disorders can result from chronic and long-term use of these drugs. Not all inhalants act alike. The abuse of different chemicals can cause damage to many different organs. In some cases, the damages have not been fully identified. This is a particular problem in inhalant abusers who abuse multiple drugs or who lack adequate nutrition and proper medical care. In this chapter, the known toxicity data will be outlined for the organs known to be at risk of damage. [28]

The nervous system is particularly susceptible to chemical abuse. Damage to the peripheral nervous system can cause numbness, weakness, and muscle paralysis. Many inhalants have been shown to damage the myelin sheath (Figure 6.1), the protective coat around nerve cells. This causes symptoms like those seen in individuals with multiple sclerosis, including abnormal fatigue, vision problems, loss of muscle coordination, slurred speech, and tremors. Direct damage to the brain

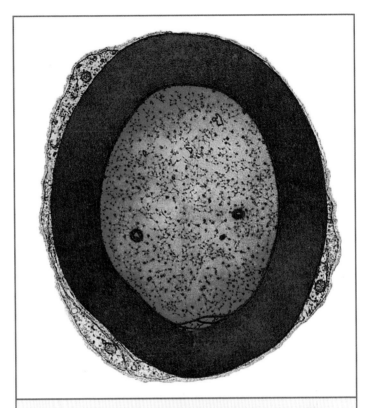

Figure 6.1 The myelin sheath, colored red in this picture, protects the spinal cord. Use of some inhalants, such as nitrous oxide, indirectly interferes with the production of the myelin sheath and, as a result, causes damage to the spinal cord.

also occurs with inhalant abuse (Figure 6.2). Research has shown atrophy, or shrinkage, of the brain's white matter with inhalant abuse. Brain damage results in impaired cognition, learning difficulties, changes in behavior and personality, problems with coordination and movement, lost or impaired sight, and hearing and memory loss.

Nitrous oxide use has been associated with damage to the nervous system and in particular the spinal cord. Nitrous oxide deactivates vitamin B_{12}, which is vital for making the sheath that protects the spinal cord. The lack of vitamin B_{12} can result in spinal cord degeneration.

Other reports have noted symptoms of numbness and weakness in the hands and legs, ataxia (the loss of ability to coordinate muscle movement), impotence, paralysis of the bladder and bowel function, personality changes, and impaired memory and intellect.

Lung inflammation, pneumonia, and other infections are frequently observed in chronic solvent abusers. Inhalant abuse can cause chemical pneumonitis, in which the lungs swell and fluid builds up in them. This can cause breathing difficulties, scarring of the lung tissue, and in some cases, death. Inhalant abuse is also linked with the development of Goodpasture's syndrome, a disorder causing hemorrhaging of the membranes lining the lungs and the kidneys. If undiagnosed and untreated, Goodpasture's syndrome can be fatal.

The heart is also a target of inhalant toxicity. Abnormal heart rhythms are associated with inhalant abuse, which can result in sudden death. This is described later in this chapter.

Liver function is often abnormal in chronic inhalant abusers. After abstinence, function usually returns to normal, but if the individual returns to inhalant use, the problems will return. When inhalant use is coupled with alcohol abuse, which also causes liver toxicity, additive effects may occur.

Inhalant abuse can result in kidney stones, severe kidney damage, and acute kidney failure. Electrolyte imbalances can occur in the kidneys and individuals may have difficulties urinating. In severely affected patients, this results in mental confusion, muscle weakness, nausea, and vomiting. Goodpasture's syndrome and glomerulonephritis, a chronic form of kidney disease, may also occur.

Exposure to nitrites appears to be associated with tumor incidence and infectious disease in animals. In humans, volatile nitrite use has been associated with Kaposi's sarcoma, a cancer that commonly occurs with AIDS. Researchers hypothesize

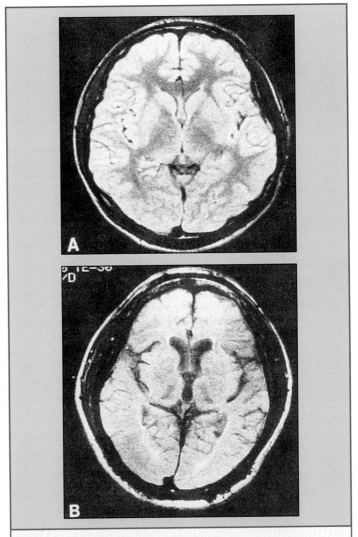

Figure 6.2 In addition to the temporary effects that inhalants can have on the body, research has shown that inhalants' abuse can also have lasting effects. The brain images shown here are evidence of the brain damage that can be caused by inhalants' abuse. Image A shows the brain of a healthy individual. In image B, which shows the brain of a person who has abused inhalants, note the shrunken white matter.

that nitrite use may contribute to the development of this cancer. Research also indicates that nitrites damage and impair the immune system, decreasing its ability to counter disease.

Some inhalants show toxicity to blood and bone marrow. Benzene is a solvent that is very toxic to bone marrow. It can cause leukemia and severe anemia. Nitrous oxide does damage to bone marrow in chronic users. Another chemical in inhalants, methylene chloride, is converted to carbon monoxide in the body. Carbon monoxide can prevent the transport of oxygen in the blood and result in brain damage.

SEXUALLY TRANSMITTED DISEASES
Nitrites, which are mainly abused by older adolescents and adults, are typically used to enhance sexual function and pleasure. The use of these drugs has been shown to be associated with unsafe sexual practices. These practices put the users at a greater risk for contracting and spreading sexually transmitted diseases such as HIV and hepatitis.

INHALANT ABUSE AND PREGNANCY
Women who are pregnant and inhalant abusers are at a heightened risk of kidney damage. Inhalant abuse also puts the developing fetus at high risk for a condition known as "fetal solvent syndrome." Case reports of newborns with fetal solvent syndrome have shown that prenatal exposure to inhalants (toluene and trichloroethylene) can results in lower birth weights, skeletal abnormalities, and delayed neurological and behavioral development. At this time, there is little known about the consequences of the abuse of specific chemicals and links to particular birth defects, but because of the potential for serious consequences of inhalant abuse, pregnant women are advised to avoid exposure to inhalants.

ADDICTION
As discussed in Chapter 5, addiction to inhalants is a disease that interferes with and eventually overwhelms the abuser's

life. The abuser spirals into needing inhalants and becomes addicted to the drug. Despite the consequences, such as loss of a job, spouse, or health, the addict will continue to seek the drug out of this necessity.

DEPRESSION AND SUICIDE

The euphoria of the high a user experiences from inhalants is short-lived. The high ultimately ends, and may be followed by an even more intense low. This low is described in the following quotation from William James:

> This instantaneous revulsion of mood from rapture to horror is, perhaps, the strongest emotion I have ever experienced. I got it repeatedly when the inhalation was continued long enough to produce incipient nausea; and I cannot but regard it as the normal and inevitable outcome of the intoxication, if sufficiently prolonged. A pessimistic fatalism, depth within depth of impotence and indifference, reason and silliness united, not in a higher synthesis, but in the fact that whichever you choose it is all one—this is the upshot of a revelation that began so rosy bright.[29]

Abuse of gases and solvents can cause severe mood swings and bouts of depression. When an individual is already struggling to cope and unhappy, the "pessimistic fatalism" may take hold and convince the individual that his life is no longer worth living. Abusers of inhalants are at a higher risk of committing suicide than individuals who do not use inhalants.

DEATH

Sudden sniffing deaths have occurred in many first-time users of inhalants, highlighting the dangers of trying these drugs. Sniffing chemicals in solvents and aerosol inhalants depresses the central nervous system and causes the heart to beat slowly and irregularly. On top of this, users may have a rush of the

PHYSICAL AND LONG-TERM CONSEQUENCES OF INHALANT ABUSE

Death—sudden sniffing deaths, suicide, cardiac arrest, suffocation, choking, respiratory arrest, injuries

Addiction

Brain damage and shrinkage

Spinal cord damage

Impaired learning and cognition

Memory loss

Personality and behavior changes

Problems with coordination and movement

Loss of vision or impaired vision

Impaired hearing

Peripheral nervous system damage

Muscle paralysis, weakness, numbness

Abnormal heart rhythms

Scarred lung tissue, impaired breathing, chemical pneumonitis

Goodpasture's syndrome

Hand tremors

Weight loss

Liver toxicity and disease (Glomerulonephritis)

Kidney damage or failure, kidney stones, electrolyte imbalance

Sores or rash on face

Leukemia

Anemia

Damage to bone marrow

Impaired immune system

Developmental harm to newborns

hormone adrenaline, produced in response to fear, surprise, stress, or excitement. Hallucinations caused by the drug, or fear of being caught or confronted by a figure of authority, may result in a rush of adrenaline during inhalant use. Adrenaline can cause the heart to experience an even more irregular rhythm, called cardiac arrhythmia, to the point that the heart may stop beating. At this point, blood and oxygen will no longer reach the brain. There are no warning signs that cardiac arrhythmia will occur, and stopping inhalation once an arrhythmia begins in many cases does not cause the arrhythmia to stop. It may be dangerous to intervene with a sniffer during use because of the risk of producing stress or fear.

Sudden sniffing deaths are responsible for more than half of the deaths due to inhalant abuse. This has been compared to a form of Russian roulette by Harvey Weiss, director of the National Inhalant Prevention Coalition, in which users may die the first time they sniff, or the tenth time, or the hundredth time. If a sniffer has used inhalants before without consequence, that does not mean she does not have a chance of experiencing a cardiac arrhythmia. Sudden sniffing deaths are mostly associated with aerosols, butane, toluene, and propane.

Inhalant use can also cause deaths by suffocation and anoxia (complete lack of oxygen). In these cases, oxygen is displaced from the lungs by the inhaled chemical. Without any oxygen reaching the brain, breathing ceases. Suffocation is most often the result of breathing from a paper or plastic bag placed over the head or attached to the mouth and nose. Some inhalants coat the lungs and make breathing difficult, or lower the levels of oxygen in the blood (hypoxia). This danger is the reason for the label warnings on aerosols and solvents to use these products in well-ventilated areas. Even when using these products for their legitimate purposes, users are warned to prevent overexposure to solvent fumes.

Vagal inhibition is another direct cause of death in inhalant users that results from inhalation of cold gases from aerosol propellants. When these gases are sprayed directly into the mouth, the larynx is stimulated by the cold substance and leads to a reflex inhibition of the heart. As a result, the heart will either slow down or may stop beating completely, causing death. In some cases, deaths have occurred by suffocation because the throat freezes due to contact with the cold substance, and the user cannot breathe and dies. In nonfatal cases, the low temperatures of the gases can cause frostbite and severe tissue damage.

Since volatile solvents depress the central nervous system, including the respiratory center of the brain, prolonged use can be hazardous. Respiratory depression can progress to respiratory arrest, in which the user stops breathing and dies. Death by choking is another possibility. Some users of inhalants have choked to death on their own vomit.

Deaths from injuries are also common. Inhalants impair judgment and can cause the user to become careless or aggressive. As with other drugs of abuse, driving while under the influence is dangerous. A sniffer may think he is invincible, have unnatural self-confidence, or have hallucinations that he can fly, for example. Sniffers have died attempting to jump from large heights, off buildings, and in front of trains, for these reasons. Another common accident occurs when someone lights a cigarette when friends are huffing flammable substances such as butane and gasoline. Many sniffers have been severely burned or killed in this type of accident. [30]

INHALANTS AS A "GATEWAY" DRUG

Inhalants were historically used as alternatives when other drugs were inaccessible or overpriced. This is also true today. Young people turn to inhalants because they are readily accessible and inexpensive. A young person may not be able to get alcohol, cigarettes, or marijuana, but inhalants are easy to buy. Two common names for inhalants are "hippie crack" and "poor man's pot," implying they are substitutes for other drugs that are out of reach.

Inhalants are considered a "gateway drug," meaning the use of the drug can open a gate to the abuse of other drugs later in life. Inhalant use is known to decrease with age. For other drugs such as alcohol and tobacco, this trend is the opposite, with use increasing with age. Instead, inhalant users may turn to other drugs as they grow older, and can legally buy alcohol and cigarettes and have greater access to illegal drugs such as marijuana, cocaine, and heroin. When a young person begins using inhalants, his or her first taste of drug use can lead to prolonged use, dependence, and addiction to drugs though life.

SOCIAL CONSEQUENCES

Because of their mood-altering properties, inhalants (and other drugs) are often used to avoid problems. The drug user may have maladaptive behavior when coping with adverse situations and emotional difficulties. An inhalant abuser will turn to drugs instead of learning to handle his emotions and make thoughtful and responsible decisions. This can become a mental and emotional crutch that hinders personal growth.

7

Trends and Use of Inhalants

GEOGRAPHICAL REGIONS

The abuse of inhalants, particularly among youths, has become a health problem for many countries. Inhalant use has been reported in many areas of the world, including the United States, Canada, Mexico, Japan, Sweden, India, England, Nigeria, Australia, Denmark, South Africa, Finland, Poland, Peru, Bulgaria, Hungary, Ireland, Rhodesia, Italy, Columbia, France, Malaysia, Scotland, Brazil, Wales, Germany, Norway, Thailand, Cuba, and New Zealand. The problem of inhalant abuse is not bounded by any local or national border.

Inhalant abuse occurs in populated urban areas, the suburbs, and isolated regions. Some of the worst outbreaks of inhalant use in the United States have been in isolated communities such as American Indian villages and sparsely populated rural areas, as well as in small border communities along the U.S.-Mexico border. In 2000, Sheshatshui, Canada, experienced an epidemic crisis of gasoline sniffing among the native Innu community. Children as young as six years old were openly sniffing gasoline poured into plastic bags. The problems in the isolated village ran much deeper than gas sniffing. The living conditions were poor and there was little meaningful employment for residents. Alcohol abuse and family dysfunction were widespread, with many parents not noticing their children were sniffing because they were abusing alcohol themselves. When the traditional Innu way of life was destroyed by historical colonization earlier in the

20th century, the entire population was demoralized and turned to self-destruction in the form of alcohol and drug abuse. After the community pleaded for outside assistance, many youth were removed from the region for treatment and detoxification because there were no adequate treatment facilities nearby.[31]

CHARACTERISTICS OF INHALANT ABUSERS

Inhalant abusers come from all walks of life. The one common factor to characterize inhalant abusers is that they are young (Figure 7.1). Some begin abusing inhalants due to peer influences or out of boredom. Some abuse inhalants to avoid their problems. Most serious abusers come from dysfunctional families with a history of addiction. Solvent abusers tend to have poor grades, and many drop out of school. Youths with an average grade of D in their last semester were over three times more likely to have used inhalants in the past year as those with an A average.[32] Whether these grades are a consequence of inhalant abuse or not is unknown. Many young abusers lack parental involvement in their life and some have a history of physical, emotional, and sexual abuse.

GENDER AND RACE/ETHNICITY

People who abuse inhalants do not fall into a specific group in terms of their gender, race, or ethnicity. In the past, solvent abusers were more often males, but in recent years, the frequency of solvent abuse between genders has equaled out. The National Household Survey on Drug Abuse (2002) reported the percentage of inhalant users by race/ethnicity in the United States as 4.0% White, 3.8% Hispanic, 2.8% Asian, and 1.6% Black (Figure 7.2).

AGE OF USERS

The most recent "Monitoring the Future Study" (2002) found that 15.2% of eighth graders, 13.5% of tenth

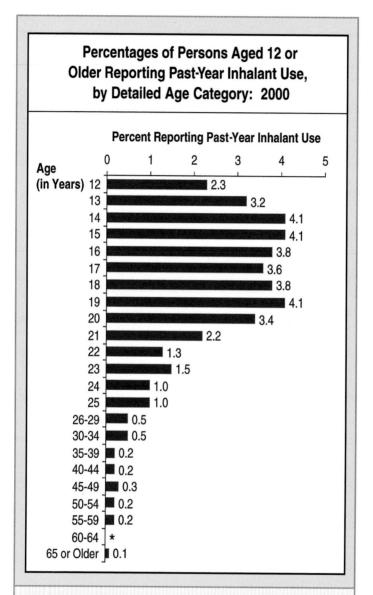

Percentages of Persons Aged 12 or Older Reporting Past-Year Inhalant Use, by Detailed Age Category: 2000

Percent Reporting Past-Year Inhalant Use

Age (in Years)

Age	Percent
12	2.3
13	3.2
14	4.1
15	4.1
16	3.8
17	3.6
18	3.8
19	4.1
20	3.4
21	2.2
22	1.3
23	1.5
24	1.0
25	1.0
26-29	0.5
30-34	0.5
35-39	0.2
40-44	0.2
45-49	0.3
50-54	0.2
55-59	0.2
60-64	*
65 or Older	0.1

Figure 7.1 Inhalant use is common in young people, particularly those between the ages of 14 and 20. Peer influence, boredom, and escapism are some of the reasons that adolescents abuse inhalants.

* No estimate reported.

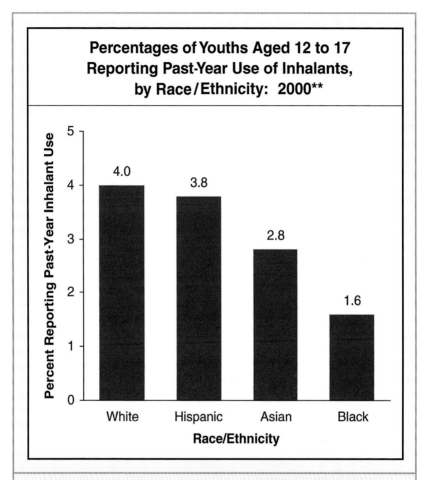

Figure 7.2 In 2000, 4% of White youths aged 12 to 17 used inhalants. This is more than twice the number of Black youths of the same age who used inhalants.

** Small sample sizes prevented comparative analysis with other racial/ethnic groups.

graders, and 11.7% of twelfth graders reported use of inhalants during their lifetime. This means that nearly one in six students in eighth grade has abused an inhalant sometime during their lifetime. During the past year, 7.7% of eighth graders, 5.8% of tenth graders, and 4.5%

of twelfth graders reported inhalant use. The annual rate of use among eighth, tenth, and twelfth graders has been declining during the past years from a peak in inhalant use reported in 1995.

Most inhalant users are initiated at a young age. In 2000, the National Household Survey on Drug Abuse found that of youths aged 12 to 15, over 2 million had used inhalants in their lifetime. Of an estimated 23 million youths, 9% had tried sniffing. Additionally, the Drug and Alcohol Services Information System Report in 2002 collected data from adolescents admitted for substance abuse treatment in 1999. Of those treated, 19% of these individuals first tried inhalants before the age of 12. Another 36% were 12 or 13, and 35% were 14 or 15.

REPEATED USE AND POPULARITY

Recent national studies have found that among youth populations, there is a surprisingly high rate of use of inhalants and that this use is frequent. Between 1994 and 2000, the National Household Survey on Drug Abuse (2001) found that the overall number of new inhalant users increased more than 50%, from 618,000 new users in 1994 to 979,000 in 2000.

PATTERNS OF USE

Most inhalant abusers are also abusing other drugs. According to the Drug and Alcohol Services Information System Report (March 2002), out of 2,091 adolescents admitted to substance-abuse programs in 1999 reporting use of inhalants, only 569 reported inhalant abuse as their primary problem. More than half of the inhalant abusers reported use of both alcohol and marijuana. Primary inhalant abusers were 0.4% of the total reported admissions for any type of substance abuse. This makes the interactions between drugs an important area for further study.

HARMLESS FUN?

The perception that inhalants are not drugs must be countered. The giggle after inhaling nitrous oxide or the euphoria felt after sniffing gasoline can bring temporary pleasure. The fact remains that the recreational abuse of inhalants is anything but harmless.

Parents and family members who have lost a loved one to inhalant addiction or inhalant experimentation are some of the strongest advocates for inhalant education. They know the tragedy that can occur from inhalant abuse firsthand.

A SHORT-LIVED PHENOMENON?

Traditionally, inhalant abuse has been seen as a transitory behavior in early adolescence. Recent data, however, have shown that this is not the case. In examining data from the National Household Survey on Drug Abuse on over 34,000 adolescents, aged 12 to 17, researchers found that first experimentation with inhalants occurs throughout adolescence. The frequency of use of inhalants extended into the late teen years, and sometimes it extended into adulthood. To consider inhalant use to occur only during a short period in early adolescence is inaccurate and under-states the breadth of inhalant use.

RELATIONSHIP TO USE OF OTHER DRUGS

Early experimentation with inhalants is strongly associated with future use of other drugs. Marijuana has most frequently been considered a "marker" for later drug use, but inhalants are evidenced to be an even better indicator of future drug use. According to Melanie Bennett and colleagues, in a study at the University of Maryland School of Medicine and the University of New Mexico, early use of inhalants confers the greatest risk for future drug use. Over a four-year period, they surveyed 3,622 undergraduates who attended a large south-western United States university for their drug-use behaviors.

A group of students who reported an early use of inhalants (before age 18) were compared with two other groups: one reporting early use of marijuana (but not inhalants), and a second group reporting no early use of either inhalants or marijuana.

The group of early inhalant users showed the highest frequency of heavy and binge drinking and drug use. These rates were substantially higher than for the group of early marijuana users. Both early inhalant and early marijuana users had a greater frequency of drug use than the group of students reporting no early experience with either drug. Many early inhalant users also had experiences with other drugs in addition to inhalants before the age of 18, such as marijuana (88%), cocaine (33%), amphetamines (58%), and hallucinogens (61%). The use of inhalants alone is very rare, so inhalant use seems to be an indicator that an individual may be using multiple drugs and may be more likely to participate in risky drinking and drug-use behavior in college.

POPULAR CULTURE AND THE MEDIA

Inhalants have made their way into the public spotlight more frequently in the last decade. For instance, inhalant abuse has been demonstrated in a number of recent movies. In the adaptation of John Irving's novel, *The Cider House Rules* (2000), Dr. William Larch, played by Michael Caine, faces a debilitating ether addiction. In *The Basketball Diaries* (1995), Leonardo DiCaprio plays Jim Carroll, an adolescent who uses inhalants and other drugs and tailspins into years of drug use. *Kids* (1996) depicts abusers inhaling vaporized butane lighter fuel from balloons. One of the first scenes of *Life as a House* (2001) shows Hayden Christensen's character Sam spraying pantyhose, stuffing them in a bag, and inhaling to get high.

The media coverage of inhalant abuse has grown in

recent years, highlighting both the lack of knowledge about inhalants and the struggle to educate on the subject. The box on pages 78–79 contains a number of 2003 headlines on inhalant abuse.

GROUPS AND SOLITARY USE

Approximately 60% of inhalant users sniff in groups.[33] For many adolescents, this is primarily a group activity, taking place with friends, siblings, or a girlfriend or boyfriend. Users may share their hallucinations with one another while sniffing to enhance the euphoric, mystical, and dreamlike experience. Communicating hallucinations can serve as a center for group rituals. For most inhalant users, the social component of drug use is very important.

Particular inhalants and methods of inhalation appear to gain popularity over others in communities due to the introduction of the product from other users. Specific locations and times for sniffing are observed by groups. Group inhalant use has been characterized as a means of expressing solidarity with the group. Individuals who want to gain acceptance in the group will experience peer pressure to sniff.

Studies have shown that as users grow older and involvement with inhalants grows, users are more likely to use inhalants by themselves.[34] These users may be initiated to sniffing in a group, but then begin sniffing alone because of a persistent need to sniff. In some cases, this may be compared to an occasional social drinker versus a chronic alcoholic. As with drinking, the solitary use of inhalants has been associated with greater dependence and psychological problems.

ATTEMPTING TO QUIT

When interviewed in treatment facilities, most inhalant users indicate that they want to stop using inhalants.[35] Most users try to quit, noting the undesirable effects, fear, and problems with family and school that result from the use of inhalants. They recognize the dangers of inhalant use, and some would prefer other drugs if they had a choice. Additionally, most users (60%) believe inhalant use is addicting. Chronic users

RECENT HEADLINES ON INHALANT ABUSE

"Students caught sniffing carburetor fluid." News 9 (San Antonio, TX), October 30, 2003.

"Innu chief seeks help for gas-sniffing youths: Labrador community built by Ottawa desperately needs addictions treatment." *The Guardian* (Charlottetown, Prince Edward Island), October 28, 2003.

"New police powers to curb 'chroming.'" ABC Online (Australia), Oct 27, 2003.

"Irish teens are tops for sniffing glue; Solvent abuse here is the worst in Europe." *The Mirror* (UK), October 23, 2003.

"Solvent abuse puts teens at risk." BBC News (UK), October 22, 2003.

"Premier steps into petrol-sniffing crisis." *Sunday Times* (Australia), October 14, 2003.

"Poppers regaining popularity." *The Toronto Star*, October 10, 2003.

"Everyday products can offer highs." *Richmond Times Dispatch* (Virginia), September 21, 2003.

"N.C. teenager may have been huffing gasoline; Police say empty can found next to body; Report still pending." *Knoxville News-Sentinel* (Tennessee), September 6, 2003.

experience withdrawal symptoms, such as shaking, headaches, chills, hallucinations, and abdominal pains. Withdrawal symptoms occur in approximately 50% to 60% of inhalant users. Relapse rates are very high in patients who have abused inhalants.

"Kenya; Government Warn Traders Selling Glue to Street Children." *Africa News*, August 22, 2003.

"Tales of abuse: Waiting to inhale; Denver area no. 1 in paint, glue sniffing, but ranks low overall." *Rocky Mountain News* (Denver, CO), August 27, 2003.

"Youth solvent abuse soars." *Sunday Herald Sun* (Melbourne, Australia), August 17, 2003.

"Boy dies sniffing $6.95 can of lighter gas." *The New Zealand Herald*, August 5, 2003.

"'Huffing' may be linked to teens' crash; Salisbury chief: Focus is on containers in car. Contents undisclosed." *Morning Call* (Allentown, PA), June 11, 2003.

"Huff and puff and blow your brains out." *Boston Globe*, May 4, 2003.

"Nitrous oxide no laughing matter." *Truth* (Auckland, New Zealand), May 2, 2003.

"Dangers of huffing hit home after teen's death." *Post and Courier* (Charleston, SC), April 24, 2003.

"Huffing: California lawsuit for selling dangerous items to children." ABC News Transcripts, *Good Morning America–ABC*, April 23, 2003.

8

Treatment
and Prevention

"Inhalant abuse is not something that's going to go away. It is prevalent in rural, urban and suburban communities across all socioeconomic lines. Once a practice like this gets entrenched in any society or community, it's virtually impossible to extinguish it. The best we can do is safeguard our communities through aggressive education of parents and children."

—**Dr. Richard Heiss**[36]

INHALANTS AND THE LAW

Most abused inhalants are legally sold products that are not intended to be inhaled and abused. In contrast to illicit drugs, there is little or no criminal involvement with the supply and possession of inhalants. Because these products are all safe when used for their intended purposes, it is impossible to control inhalant abuse by eliminating the availability of inhalants. Bulk supplies of acetone, diethyl ether, and toluene are under international control, but this does not affect the availability of the household products containing these chemicals.

Most of the common household and commercial products abused as inhalants are not regulated under the Controlled Substances Act or any other national law in the United States. As a result, many state legislatures have attempted to deter youths from abusing them by placing restrictions on their sale to minors. During the 1990s, 38 states adopted laws preventing the sale, use, and/or distribution of various products commonly abused as inhalants to minors to

Figure 8.1 Most inhalants are products that are sold legally and that are not intended to be inhaled or abused. To prevent youths from abusing these products, many states have adopted laws to prevent the sale of these products to minors. In some stores, spray paint is stored behind a cage and is not accessible to consumers unless they have proper identification.

prevent use of these products as drugs. In many states, the sale, transfer, or offer of products containing inhalants to a minor is a crime. Identification may be required for the sale of certain products.

One example is spray paints sold in hardware stores, which are often caged and inaccessible to consumers lacking proper identification (Figure 8.1). Preventing minors from purchasing spray paint is one way to curb inhalant abuse.

In some states, possession of an intoxicant and inhaling specific compounds for intoxication are crimes. Additionally, inhalant intoxication in some cases is prosecuted under DUI (driving under the influence) laws, if the user operates a motor vehicle while under the influence of an inhalant.

The specific chemicals prohibited differ from state to state, as does the punishment. Violation of inhalant laws may result in a fine and/or jail time, depending on the state where the violation occurred. Three states, New Mexico, Maine, and New Hampshire, offer a treatment option for violators.

In England and Wales, volatile substances are controlled under the Intoxicating Substances Supply Act of 1985. Similar legislation was passed in Scotland. This Act makes it illegal for a retailer to supply or offer to supply, to a young person under the age of 18, a substance that the supplier knows or has reason to believe will be used "to achieve intoxication."

In the United States and Canada there are also examples of regulated access to gasoline in local areas where gasoline is heavily abused. In these cases, gasoline tanks are buried or caged to prevent misuse.

SCHOOL-ENFORCED RULES

Schools may enforce their own rules regarding inhalants. In some cases, liquid correction fluid has been banned from schools. Varieties of correction fluid have been adapted by some manufacturers to minimize the toxic solvent components as a result. In some schools, even nail polish is banned, to prevent users from sniffing the polish. Art classroom markers, rubber cement, and paints may also be monitored.

DRUG TESTING

Drug tests are infrequently used to detect inhalant abuse. More often, a diagnosis is made after physical symptoms of inhalant abuse are noticed or become apparent (intoxication, chemical smell on breath and clothing, weight loss, and illness), and the diagnosis is made by a physician. There is no standard drug test available to detect the use of inhalants because of the sheer number of chemicals abused.

There are six primary types of drug tests used: urine, breath, blood, hair, saliva, and sweat. The most common drug test used is the urine test. Laboratory confirmation of inhalant abuse can be difficult because the parent compound is broken down (except in the case of acetone). Due to this breakdown, the abused inhalant is weakly represented in the urine. Instead, drug tests look for the breakdown products or metabolites of the inhalants, which allows for detection of inhalant exposure over a number of days. This has long been used to monitor workplace exposure to volatile solvents for employees in industrial factories. For example, the test for toluene exposure looks for hippuric acid, the major breakdown product of toluene. Blood samples are more expensive and difficult to collect, but are the sample of choice to indicate use of or intoxication by inhalants. With blood samples, raised liver enzymes (needed to breakdown the inhaled chemicals) suggest inhalant abuse even if the drug and metabolite are not directly detected. In addition, breath samples may be used for inhalant detection. Though testing breath samples is convenient, there is a limited window of time for detection, from a few hours to a few days (in chronic abusers).

TREATMENT

The major form of inhalant-abuse treatment is detoxification and therapy in treatment programs. Detoxifying users who huff or sniff inhalants can take months and also requires extensive counseling. Inhalants can stay in the body for weeks, necessitating a long detoxification period, and abusers are often unable to begin therapy until detoxification is complete.

Therapy for an inhalant abuser, as with other drug abusers, is required for as long as a two-year period. Because counselors have noted that inhalant abusers often have short attention spans, it is advisable that therapy begin with short sessions of 15–20 minutes, gradually progressing to longer sessions. Simple procedures and repetition may be required to ensure the client understands the discussion. Treatment clinics are also advised to ensure that there are no inhalable products on the premises and to closely monitor any necessary solvents that a patient could find and abuse during detoxification and treatment.

Since inhalant abusers typically abuse a number of types of inhalants, a thorough physical examination and detailed history of the compounds they have abused is critical. This is followed by treatments for the medical conditions that have been caused by the inhalant(s) abused. Treatment for inhalant abusers is often complicated by the fact that inhalant abusers use multiple drugs (Figure 8.2).

Treatment facilities have taken note that inhalant abusers most often do not solely abuse inhalants. In the 1999 "Treatment Episode Data Set" study by the Substance Abuse and Mental Health Services Administration (SAMHSA), 1,321 individuals were admitted for treatment of inhalant abuse. These cases, where inhalants were the primary abused drug, accounted for only 0.1% of admittances in the treatment facilities. Often patients reported inhalant use in addition to their primary substance of abuse. One-third of the inhalant users admitted that they began using inhalants by age 12, and an additional 24% began using inhalants between age 12 and 14.

DIFFICULTIES IN TREATING INHALANT ABUSE

The treatment of inhalant abuse faces some serious problems. Some substance abuse clinics often do not even know how to treat inhalant abusers. It is shocking that in spite of the fact that inhalant abuse is a widespread problem, inhalant abusers are often faced with having nowhere to turn to for help. Since inhalant abuse often arises in episodic events in communities, towns facing major problems with youth abuse often find that there is nowhere to accommodate the abusers for treatment and no nearby treatment facilities that can handle detoxification specific to inhalant abuse. Some communities have faced these problems by setting up their own treatment facilities, but this takes time and money. Indeed, with time being critical for treatment of abusers who need it, the lack of adequate treatment

Figure 8.2 Abusers of inhalants often abuse other drugs, such as alcohol and marijuana. Treatment of inhalant abusers is often complicated by the fact that they use multiple varieties of inhalants and drugs.

facilities has led to emergencies, with local areas begging for outside help.

Instead, most programs are better funded and equipped for other drugs of abuse, adult patients, and patients who enter treatment programs of their own will. Often, treatment program workers have not been trained to work with inhalant users in the community and outside of health centers, where treatment is thought to be more effective.

Studies by SAMHSA and the National Institute on Drug Abuse (NIDA) have shown that inhalant abusers often have problems in addition to the abuse of multiple drugs. Inhalant abusers often have family problems, poor self-esteem, personality disorders, cognitive impairment, and mental illness. Staff members of treatment programs have repeatedly charac-terized inhalant users with words such as "psychologically maladjusted, ego weakness, personality disorganization, poor impulse control, low frustration tolerance, withdrawn, uninterested, destructive, overactive, restless, disruptive and lacking discipline."[37] Many inhalant abusers have poor academic records and exceptionally high expulsion rates from school, and are more likely than the average student to drop out of school. Some of these problems may have contributed to the use of inhalants as an escape, and some may be the consequence of inhalant abuse causing detrimental changes in a young person's life.

This combination of multiple neurological, psychological, and social problems makes chronic inhalant abusers a very unique and difficult treatment group. Each individual patient has a unique set of behavioral problems and combination of inhalants and/or other drugs abused. Treatment for inhalant abuse must resolve some of these problems or help the patient cope with problems without turning to drugs.

Keeping inhalant users in treatment for an appropriate length of time poses problems as well. When brain injury has occurred as a result of inhalant abuse, the treatment process moves at an even slower rate because of the cognitive problems the patient faces. Treatment center staff have reported difficulties in getting their clients to keep their appointments and remain in treatment programs. Outpatient programs also report difficulties in getting their clients to keep their appointments, so to counter this, staff members are generally sent into the field to do counseling.

A large contributing factor to this problem is that the clients in treatment are not always in treatment by choice. In many cases, inhalant users are referred to programs by criminal-justice agencies under emergency circumstances, such as a bad episode with inhalants. Often, inhalant users are admitted to treatment after an arrest, or treatment is a condition of their parole. Since they did not seek treatment on their own, they are often unmotivated and uninterested in the treatment program. More often than any other treatment group, inhalant users drop out or are expelled from treatment programs for noncompliance with the program rules.

TREATMENT MEDICATION

Presently, there are no treatment medications for inhalant addiction that have been approved by the Food and Drug Administration (FDA). There are medications, however, available for treating the adverse health effects of inhalants. Hopefully, research will prove to be fruitful in better understanding the mechanism of inhalant addiction and in devising a treatment medication.

EDUCATION

The third week of March has been designated as National Inhalants & Poisons Awareness Week by the National Inhalant Prevention Coalition (originally a state-wide prevention program from Texas that has grown to a national organization). This initiative provides facts and information about inhalant abuse and aims to raise awareness of the prevalence of inhalant abuse and the risks involved with using inhalants (Figure 8.3). National Inhalants & Poisons Awareness Week is a program involving youth, schools, police departments, media, and health organizations, as well as other community groups. In 2002, more than 800 organizations in 46 states participated.

In Texas, where National Inhalants & Poisons Awareness Week has been most extensively observed, inhalant use has decreased. Between 1992 and 1994, inhalant use decreased by 30% in elementary school and was reduced more than 20% at the high-school level from state agency surveys of over 176,000 students. The National Inhalant Prevention Coalition estimates that over 100,000 students who may have used inhalants chose not to, in part because of this initiative.

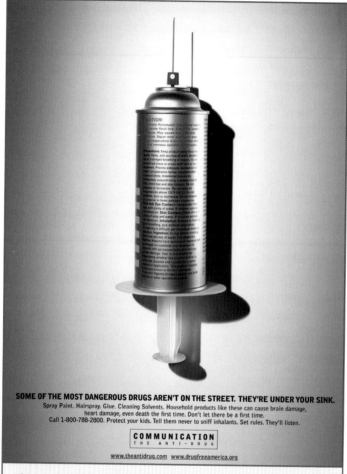

SOME OF THE MOST DANGEROUS DRUGS AREN'T ON THE STREET. THEY'RE UNDER YOUR SINK.
Spray Paint. Hairspray. Glue. Cleaning Solvents. Household products like these can cause brain damage,
heart damage, even death the first time. Don't let there be a first time.
Call 1-800-788-2800. Protect your kids. Tell them never to sniff inhalants. Set rules. They'll listen.

COMMUNICATION
THE ANTI-DRUG

www.theantidrug.com www.drugfreeamerica.org

Figure 8.3 Education is one way to discourage inhalant use and abuse. These campaigns have been shown to decrease inhalant use by raising awareness of the risks involved with abusing inhalants. Posters, such as this one, educate both parents and adolescents about the fact that common household products can have dangerous effects.

During the tenth annual National Inhalants & Poisons Awareness Week in 2002, two postcards were issued by the National Institute on Drug Abuse and the National Inhalant Prevention Coalition depicting the heart-stopping and brain-damaging effects of sniffing inhalants. The coalition sent 12,500 of these cards to surf, skate, and ski shops around the country to reach and educate teen audiences.

The organization provides kits with art materials for reproduction, sample radio and press scripts, and up-to-date statistics to help engage local communities in a comprehensive inhalant education and prevention effort.

Although parents often discuss the dangers of drinking, smoking cigarettes, and marijuana, inhalants are often overlooked. To be most effective, drug prevention should start early (before age 12) but according to the nonprofit group "Partnership for a Drug-Free America," nine out of 10 parents are unaware that their children may have ever used inhalants. This startling statistic underscores the necessity of educating parents, as well as teenagers, about inhalant use and abuse. If it is so easy for parents to miss the signs that their child has used inhalants, then it is critical to inform parents of the products abused, the trends in use, and signs of inhalant abuse. Parents should be able to recognize if their child is using inhalants, and the dangers of inhalant use should be discussed rather than overlooked.

KEYS TO SUCCESSFUL PREVENTION PROGRAMS

NIDA has identified effective and important characteristics of prevention programs for families, schools, and communities. One key point is that prevention programs should enhance "protective factors," and minimize or reverse "risk factors." Protective factors are associated with a reduced potential for drug use, and include strong and positive bonds in family, clear rules and consistent enforcement of rules within the family, monitoring by parents and involvement of parents in their children's lives, success in school, strong bonds to social organizations, and having standard ideas about the use of drugs. In contrast, risk factors are associated with an increased potential for drug use, and include chaotic home environments and homes in which parents suffer from mental illnesses or abuse drugs, ineffective parenting of children with conduct disorders or difficult temperaments, lack of attachment and nurturing within the home, inappropriately shy or aggressive behavior in the classroom, poor school performance, poor social and coping skills, socializing with peers who display deviant behavior, and holding positive perceptions of drug-use behaviors in their family, peer, work, school, and community environments.

Prevention programs can target either a variety of drugs or target a single class of drugs like inhalants. They should include training in general life skills, skills that enable an individual to resist taking drugs when offered them and strengthen an individual's personal commitments against the use of drugs. Peer and group discussion and interactive methods must be included, and these programs should be repeated throughout a student's education. Programs have a greater impact when they include a component to train parents and caregivers to reinforce what their children are learning and open a forum for family discussion.

Community programs, such as media campaigns and regulations to restrict access to drugs, are more effective when discussed by both the school and family. Prevention programs should be adapted if there are specific risks or specific drugs being used in local communities. If a population has a higher risk level, then the prevention effort must begin earlier and

FACTS ABOUT INHALANT PREVENTION AND TREATMENT

- **There are no treatment medications approved by the FDA for inhalant abuse.**

- **Most inhalant abusers believe inhalant use is addictive and have tried to quit.**

- **Nine out of 10 parents do not know that their child is abusing inhalants.**

be more intensive to be effective. NIDA has also noted that prevention programs are cost-effective when they work well. For each dollar spent on drug-use prevention, the community can save four to five dollars in drug-abuse treatment and counseling.

CONCLUSIONS

The accessibility of inhalants as a cheap and easy way to get high will not change. The chemicals in inhalants are useful and necessary in industries and in the household. There is no way to completely regulate their use or to prevent misuse. Considering this fact, education and prevention programs are the keys to eliminate abuse of these products. There is a thorough knowledge of the dangers of inhalant abuse. Deaths can occur during any episode of use by sudden sniffing death. Accidents are frequent, as with other drugs of abuse, because of impaired judgment. Organ damage is known to occur in chronic abusers, and damage to the brain can cause lifelong impairment and consequences. Learning how inhalants act at the cellular level is an area of research that has been receiving increasingly more attention, and hopefully will continue to do so.

Inhalant users use inhalants for many reasons, including their availability and affordability, the quick high they produce, the ease of hiding abuse, and the lack of criminal prosecution. Inhalant use has been correlated with the use of other drugs of abuse, which again emphasizes the importance of prevention and education. Addiction to inhalants is a disease and a serious health problem. Treatment for inhalant abusers must improve to help individuals and their families to cope with and fight the disease. There is much more information about inhalant abuse available than is covered in this book, and readers are encouraged to use the Bibliography and the Internet to continue to educate themselves about the dangers of using inhalants. An informed populace is the first step in reducing and eliminating inhalant use and abuse.

Notes

Chapter 1

1. *NIDA Research Report Series: Inhalant Abuse—Its Dangers Are Nothing to Sniff At,* 1994.
2. Sharp and Rosenberg, 1997.
3. Bennett et al., 2000.
4. Beauvais, 1992.
5. Beauvais, 1992.

Chapter 2

6. Sharp, 1992.
7. Frost, 1985.

Chapter 3

8. Balster, 1998; Layzer, 1985.
9. Layzer, 1985.
10. Balster, 1998.
11. Balster, 1998; National Institute on Drug Abuse Research Report Series: Inhalant Abuse, 2000.
12. Kerner, 1988; Sharp, 1992; Sharp and Rosenberg, 1997; National Institute on Drug Abuse Research Report Series: Inhalant Abuse, 2000.
13. Mason, 1979. Kerner, 1988
14. Tgmoczko, 1996.
15. James, 1990.
16. Sharp and Rosenberg, 1997.

Chapter 4

17. Evans and Balster, 1991; National Institute on Drug Abuse Research Report Series: Inhalants, 2000.
18. Gerasimov et al., 2002.
19. Riegel and French, 2002.

Chapter 5

20. Ramos, 1998.
21. Mason, 1979.

22. Grosse and Grosse, 2000.
23. American Psychiatric Association, *Diagnostic and Statistical Manual of Mental Disorders,* 4th ed., 1994.
24. Spiess, 2001.
25. Layzer, 1985.
26. Mason, 1979.

Chapter 6

27. Becker, 1980.
28. *Beyond the ABCs: Solvents/Inhalants,* 1998; Brodsky, 1985; "Inhalants." *Substance Abuse Treatment Advisory: Breaking News from the Treatment Field,* 2003; Layzer, 1985; National Institute on Drug Abuse Research Report Series: Inhalant Abuse, 2000; Rosenberg and Sharp, 1992; Sharp and Rosenberg, 1997.
29. James, 1990.
30. "Inhalants." *Substance Abuse Treatment Advisory: Breaking News from the Treatment Field,* 2003.

Chapter 7

31. Rowland, 2000.
32. National Household Survey of Drug Abuse, 2002.
33. Mason, 1979.
34. Mason, 1979; Sharp, 1992.
35. Mason, 1979.

Chapter 8

36. Heiss, 2002.
37. Mason, 1979.

Bibliography

American Psychiatric Association. *Diagnostic and Statistical Manual of Mental Disorders, Fourth Edition-Revised (DSM-IV)*. Washington, D.C.: American Psychiatric Association, 1994.

Ball, P. (July 17, 2001) "Oracle's Secret Fault Found." *Nature Science Update*. Retrieved March 25, 2003. Available online at: *http://www.nature.com/nsu/010719/010719-10.html*.

Balster, R.L. "Neural Basis of Inhalant Abuse." *Drug and Alcohol Dependence* 51 (1998): 207–214.

Beauvais, F. "Volatile Solvent Abuse: Trends and Patterns," *Inhalant Abuse: A Volatile Research Agenda*, eds. C.W. Sharp, F. Beauvais, and R. Spence. Research Monograph 129. NIH Pub. No. 93–3475. Rockville, MD: National Institute on Drug Abuse, 1992, pp. 13–42.

Becker, H.S. "The Social Basis of Drug-Induced Experiences." *Theories on Drug Abuse: Selected Contemporary Perspectives.*, eds. D. J. Lettieri, M. Sayers, and H. Wallenstein. National Institute on Drug Abuse Research Monograph No. 30. DHEW Pub. No. (ADM) 80–967. Washington, D.C.: Supt. of Docs., U.S. Govt. Printing Office, 1980. pp. 180–190.

Beckstead, M.J., R. Phelan, and S.J. Mihic. "Antagonism of Inhalant and Volatile Anesthetic Enhancement of Glycine Receptor Function." *Journal of Biological Chemistry* 276 (2001): 24959–24964.

Beckstead, M.J., J.L. Weiner, E.I. Eger II, D.H. Gong, and S.J. Mihic. "Glycine and Gamma-aminobutyric acid(A) Receptor Function is Enhanced by Inhaled Drugs of Abuse." *Molecular Pharmacology* 57 (2000): 1199–1205.

Bennett, M.E., S.T. Walters, J.H. Miller, and W.G. Woodall. "Relationship of Early Inhalant Use to Substance Abuse in College Students." *Journal of Substance Abuse* 12 (2000): 227–240.

Beyond the ABCs: Solvents/Inhalants. Information for Professionals. Edmonton, Alberta: Alberta Alcohol and Drug Abuse Commission, 1998.

Brecher, E.M. and the editors of Consumer Reports. *Licit and Illicit Drugs: The Consumer Union Report on Narcotics, Stimulants, Depressants, Inhalants, Hallucinogens, and Marijuana—Including Caffeine, Nicotine and Alcohol*. Boston: Little, Brown and Company, 1972, pp. 309–34.

Brodsky, J.B. "Toxicity of Nitrous Oxide," *Nitrous Oxide/N2O*, eds. E.I. Eger II, M.D., ed. New York: Elsevier Science Publishing Company, 1985, pp. 259–279.

Cohen, H. "Inhalants: Legal, Possibly Lethal and Very Addictive." *The Scientist* 16 (2002): 7.

Cruz, S.L., R.L. Balster, and J.J. Woodward. "Effects of Volatile Solvents on Recombinant N-methyl-D-aspartate Receptors Expressed in Xenopus Oocytes." *British Journal of Pharmacology* 131(2000): 1303–1308.

Bibliography

Cruz, S.L., T. Mirshahi, B. Thomas, R.L. Balster, and J.J. Woodward. "Effects of the Abused Solvent Toluene on Recombinant NMDA and Non-NMDA Receptors Expressed in Xenopus Oocytes." *Journal of Pharmacology and Experimental Therapeutics* 286 (1998): 334–340.

The DASIS Report: Adolescent Admissions Involving Inhalants. Rockville, MD.: Office of Applied Studies, Substance Abuse and Mental Health Administration, 2002.

De Boer, J.Z., J.R. Hale, and J. Chanton. "New Evidence of the Geological Origins of the Ancient Delphic Oracle (Greece)." *Geology* 29 (2001): 707–710.

Evans, E.B., and R.L. Balster. "CNS Depressant Effects of Volatile Organic Solvents." *Neuroscience Biobehavior Review* 15 (1991): 233–241.

Evans, E.B., and R.L. Balster. "Inhaled 1,1,1-Trichloroethane-produced Physical Dependence in Mice: Effect of Drugs and Vapors on Withdrawal." *Journal of Pharmacology and Experimental Therapeutics* 264 (1993): 726–733.

Feldman, R.S., S.M. Jerrold, and L.F. Quenzer. *Principles of Neuropsychopharmacology.* Sunderland, MA: Sinauer Associates, Inc., Publishers, 1997.

Fenster, J. M. *Ether Day: The Strange Tale of America's Greatest Medical Discovery and the Haunted Men Who Made It.* New York: HarperCollins Publishers Inc., 2001.

Flanagan, R.J., P.J. Streete, and J.D. Ramsey. "Volatile Substance Abuse: Practical Guidelines for Analytical Investigation of Suspected Cases and Interpretation of Results." *UNDCP Technical Series,* No. 5. Vienna, Austria: United Nations Office on Drugs and Crime, 1997.

Frost, E. A.M. "A History of Nitrous Oxide." In: E. I. Eger II, M.D., ed. *Nitrous Oxide/N2O.* New York: Elsevier Science Publishing Company, 1985, pp. 1–22.

Gerasimov, M.R., R.A. Ferrieri, W.K. Schiffer, J. Logan, S.J. Gatley, A.N. Gifford, D.A. Alexoff, D.A. Marsteller, C. Shea, V. Garza, P. Carter, P. King, C.R. Ashby, Jr., S. Vitkun, and S.L. Dewey. "Study of Brain Uptake and Biodistribution of [^{11}C]Toluene in Non-Human Primates and Mice." *Life Sciences* 70(2002): 2811–2828.

Gerasimov, M.R., W.K. Schiffer, D. Marstellar, R. Ferrieri, D. Alexoff, and S.L. Dewey. "Toluene Inhalation Produces Regional Specific Changes in Extracellular Dopamine." *Drug and Alcohol Dependence* 65 (2002): 243–251.

Grosse, K., and J. Grosse. "Propane Abuse: Extreme Dose Due to the Development of Tolerance." *Nervenarzt* 71 (2000): 50–53.

Hanson, G. R. *Rising to the Challenges of Inhalant Abuse.* NIDA Notes, Director's Column. Vol. 17, No. 4. Rockville, MD: National Institute on Drug Abuse, 2002.

Heiss, R. (11/15/2002) "Tragedy in the Household—An Interview with Dr. Richard Heiss." *Drug Story.* [online] Retrieved April 29, 2003. Available online at *http://www.drugstory.org/feature/drrichard.asp.*

"Inhalant Abuse." *Drug Testing Quarterly.* Flagstaff, AZ: Norchem Drug Testing Laboratory, 2001, pp. 1–2.

Inhalants Prevention-Parent's Guide. New York: Partnership for a Drug-Free America, 2003.

"Inhalants." *Substance Abuse Treatment Advisory: Breaking News for the Treatment Field.* Volume 3, Issue 1. Rockville, MD: Center for Substance Abuse Treatment, 2003.

"Inhalants Revisited: An Update." *Health and Health Care in Schools.* Vol. 3, No. 3, Washington, D.C.: Center for Health and Health Care in Schools, 2002.

James, W. *The Varieties of Religious Experience.* New York: Vintage Books, 1990.

Kerner, K. "Current Topics in Inhalant Abuse," *Epidemiology of Inhalant Abuse: An Update,* eds. R.A. Crider and B.A. Rouse. Research Monograph 85. DHHS Pub. No. (ADM)88–1577. Rockville, MD: National Institute on Drug Abuse, 1988, pp. 8–29.

Layzer, R.B. "Nitrous Oxide Abuse," *Nitrous Oxide/N2O,* ed. E.I. Eger II, M.D. New York: Elsevier Science Publishing Company, 1985, pp. 249–257.

Mason, T. *Inhalant Use and Treatment.* Services Research Monograph Series. DHEW Pub No. (ADM)79–783. Rockville, MD: National Institute on Drug Abuse, 1979.

Mihic, S.J., Q.Ye, M.J. Wick, V.V. Koltchine, M.D. Krasowski, S.E. Finn, M.P. Mascia, C.F. Valenzuela, K.K. Hanson, E.P. Greenblatt, R.A. Harris, and N.L. Harrison, "Sites of Alcohol and Volatile Anaesthetic Action on GABA(A) and Glycine Receptors." *Nature* 389 (1997): 385–389.

Monitoring the Future: 2002 Data From In-School Surveys of 8th, 10th, and 12th Grade Students. Ann Arbor, MI: Substance Abuse and Mental Health Data Archive, the Inter-university Consortium for Political and Social Research and the University of Michigan, 2002.

Nagle, D.R. "Anesthetic Addiction and Drunkenness." *International Journal of the Addictions* 3 (1968): 33.

National Institute on Drug Abuse InfoFacts: Drug Addiction Treatment Medications. Rockville, MD: National Institute on Drug Abuse, 2003.

Bibliography

National Institute on Drug Abuse InfoFacts: Lessons from Prevention Research. Rockville, MD: National Institute on Drug Abuse, 2003.

National Institute on Drug Abuse Research Report Series: Inhalant Abuse. Rockville, MD: National Institute on Drug Abuse, 2000.

National Institute on Drug Abuse Research Report Series: Inhalant Abuse—Its Dangers Are Nothing to Sniff At. Rockville, MD: National Institute on Drug Abuse, 1994.

The NHSDA Report: Inhalant Use Among Youths. Rockville, MD: Office of Applied Studies, Substance Abuse and Mental Health Administration, 2002.

Oetting, E.R., R.W. Edwards, and F. Beauvais. "Social and Psychological Factors Underlying Inhalant Abuse," *Epidemiology of Inhalant Abuse: An Update*, eds. R.A. Crider and B.A. Rouse. Research Monograph 85. DHHS Pub. No. (ADM) 88-1577. Rockville, MD: National Institute on Drug Abuse, 1988, pp. 172–203.

Plutarch. "Obsolescence of Oracles," *Plutarch's Moralia*, Vol. 5, trans. F.C. Babbitt. Cambridge, MA: Harvard University Press, 1957, pp. 348–501.

Ramanathan, V.M., T.G. Reigle, S. Muralidhara, and C.E. Dallas. "Effects of Acute Inhalation Exposure to Isoamyl Nitrite on the Hypothala-mopituitary-Adrenal Axis in Male Sprague-Dawley Rats." *Journal of Toxicology and Environmental Health A* 55 (1988): 345–58.

Ramos, R. *An Ethnographic Study of Mexican American Inhalant Abusers in San Antonio, Texas.* Austin, TX: Texas Commission on Alcohol and Drug Abuse, 1998.

Rassool, G.H. "An Overview of Psychoactive Drugs," *Substance Use and Misuse: Nature, Context and Clinical Interventions*, eds. G.H. Rassool. Oxford: Blackwell Science, 1998, pp. 48–50.

Riegel, A.C., and E.D. French. "Abused Inhalants and Central Reward Pathways." *Ann. N.Y. Acad. Sci.* 965 (2002): 281–291.

Roach, J. (August 14, 2001) "Delphic Oracle's Lips May Have Been Loosened by Gas Vapors." *National Geographic News.* Retrieved March 25, 2003. Available online at *http://news.nationalgeographic.com/news/2001/08/0814_delphioracle.html.*

Rosenberg, N.L. and C.W. Sharp. "Solvent Toxicity: A Neurological Focus," *Inhalant Abuse: A Volatile Research Agenda*, eds. C.W. Sharp, F. Beauvais, and R. Spence. Research Monograph 129. NIH Pub. No. 93-3475. Rockville, MD: National Institute on Drug Abuse, 1992, pp. 117–171.

Rowland, R. (November 17, 2000) "Desperate Village." *CBC News Online.* Retrieved May 6, 2003. Available online at *http://www.cbc.ca/news/indepth/sheshatshiu/town.html.*

Sharp, C.W. "Introduction to Inhalant Abuse," *Inhalant Abuse: A Volatile Research Agenda*, eds. C.W. Sharp, F. Beauvais, and R. Spence. Research Monograph 129. NIH Pub. No. 93-3475. Rockville, MD: National Institute on Drug Abuse, 1992, pp. 1–11.

Sharp, C.W. and N.L. Rosenberg. "Inhalants," *Substance Abuse: A Comprehensive Textbook*, eds. J.H. Lowinson, P. Ruiz, R.B. Millman, and J.G. Langrod. Baltimore: Williams and Wilkins, 1997, pp. 246–264.

Speiss, M. *Inhalants.* Rockville, MD: ONDCP Drug Policy Information Clearinghouse Fact Sheet, 2001.

Snyder, S.H. *Drugs and the Brain.* New York: Scientific American Books, Inc., 1999.

Substance Abuse and Mental Health Services Administration, Office of Applied Studies. Treatment Episode Data Set (TEDS): 1994–1999. Rockville, MD: National Admissions to Substance Abuse Treatment Services, DASIS Series: S-14, DHHS Publication No. (SMA) 01-3550, 2001.

Tymoczko, D. "The Nitrous Oxide Philosopher." *The Atlantic Monthly.* 277 (1996): 93–101.

West, B. *APRC Fact Sheet: Inhalants.* Phoenix, AZ: Arizona Prevention Resource Center, 2001.

Further Reading

BOOKS
Nonfiction

Fenster, Julie M. *Ether Day: The Strange Tale of America's Greatest Medical Discovery and the Haunted Men Who Made It.* New York: HarperCollins Publishers, 2001.

Frey, James. *A Million Little Pieces.* New York: N.A. Talese/Doubleday, 2003.

Fiction

Carroll, Jim. *The Basketball Diaries.* New York: Penguin Books, 1978.

Faulkner, William. *The Sound and the Fury.* New York: Random House, Inc., 1929.

Irving, John. *The Cider House Rules.* New York: Morrow, 1985.

Thompson, Hunter S. *Fear and Loathing in Las Vegas: A Savage Journey To The Heart Of The American Dream.* New York: Random House, 1971.

Wodehouse, P.G. *Laughing Gas.* Garden City, NY: Doubleday, Doran & Company, Inc., 1936.

FILMS
Documentary Films

Children Underground (2001) Director: Edet Belzberg

Hillbrow Kids (1999) Directors: Jacqueline Görgen and Michael Hammon

Fiction

The Adventures of Sebastian Cole (1999) Director: Tod Williams

The Basketball Diaries (1995) Director: Scott Kalvert

Blue Velvet (1986) Director: David Lynch

Boys Don't Cry (1999) Director: Kimberly Peirce

Cider House Rules (1999) Director: Lasse Hallström

Citizen Ruth (1996) Director: Alexander Payne

Fear and Loathing in Las Vegas (1998) Director: Terry Gilliam

The Great Moment (1944) Director: Preston Sturges

Kids (1995) Director: Larry Clark

Laughing Gas (1914) Director: Charles Chaplin

Life as a House (2001) Director: Irwin Winkler

Love Liza (2002) Director: Todd Louiso

WEBSITES

National Clearinghouse for Alcohol and Drug Information

www.health.org

National Inhalant Prevention Coalition

www.inhalants.org

National Institute on Drug Abuse (NIDA)

www.drugabuse.gov, www.nida.nih.gov

National Institutes of Health

www.nih.gov

National Library of Medicine

www.nlm.nih.gov

National Youth Anti-Drug Media Campaign

www.freevibe.com

Substance Abuse and Mental Health Services Administration

www.samhsa.gov
www.findtreatment.samhsa.gov

White House Office of National Drug Control Policy

www.whitehousedrugpolicy.gov

Index

Picture Credits

About the Author

Ingrid A. Lobo was born in Hamilton, Ontario, Canada. She received her Bachelor of Science degree in Molecular Biology from the University of Texas at Austin in 1999. Currently, she is a graduate student in the Waggoner Center for Alcohol and Addiction Research at the University of Texas at Austin working towards her Ph.D. This is her first book.

About the Editor

David J. Triggle is a University Professor and a Distinguished Professor in the School of Pharmacy and Pharmaceutical Sciences at the State University of New York at Buffalo. He studied in the United Kingdom and earned his B.Sc. degree in Chemistry from the University of Southampton and a Ph.D. degree in Chemistry at the University of Hull. Following postdoctoral work at the University of Ottawa in Canada and the University of London in the United Kingdom, he assumed a position at the School of Pharmacy at Buffalo. He served as Chairman of the Department of Biochemical Pharmacology from 1971 to 1985 and as Dean of the School of Pharmacy from 1985 to 1995. From 1995 to 2001 he served as the Dean of the Graduate School, and as the University Provost from 2000 to 2001. He is the author of several books dealing with the chemical pharmacology of the autonomic nervous system and drug-receptor interactions, and some 400 scientific publications, and has delivered over 1,000 lectures worldwide on his research.